The Satirist
America's Most Critical Book

Volume 1

Dan Geddes

For Maria, for making our lives charmed and beautiful

Author's Note

Nothing in this book is real.

This book is a collection of satires, parodies, satirical news, biographies of imaginary geniuses, reviews of imaginary movies and books, and a few poems and short stories.

Each piece can be read in isolation, but there are also recurring themes.

It is all fiction of one stripe or another, often containing elements of parody and satire, even when historical persons and events are mentioned.

Much of this book appeared in earlier form in *The Satirist: America's Most Critical Journal* (www.thesatirist.com) from 1999 to 2012. Many of the pieces herein are written in the form of criticism, which is why this book is subtitled "America's Most Critical Book."

The Satirist online journal also features serious criticism of actual books and films. These will be collected in a separate volume.

Dan Geddes
12 December 2012
Amsterdam

Contents

Writing long books is a laborious and impoverishing act of foolishness: expanding in five hundred pages an idea that could be perfectly explained in a few minutes. A better procedure is to pretend that those books already exist and to offer a summary, a commentary.

—Jorge Luis Borges

Satires

The Seven Habits of Highly Efficient Cult Leaders

Techniques for creating successful religious cults have changed dramatically since the cult heyday of the 1970s.

Millions of people are desperate to find the definitive "answers" to life's big questions—even if incorrect answers—that religions and cults have always supplied.

The new millennium has opened up lucrative opportunities for cult leaders with the boldness and vision to exploit others. The rise of cable television and the Internet provide rich media to supplement the word-of-mouth buzz upon which cult formation has always relied.

The Seven Habits of Highly Efficient Cult Leaders

Grooming

Your personal appearance must be polished, at least at first. Only later can you degenerate into bad hygiene. But be careful! If you "go natural" too early in the cult's development, you will just be smelly, and will destroy your cult in its infancy.

Strength

It is wise to be physically stronger than everyone else in your cult. This gives you the appearance of vitality and makes others look up to you. It's also helpful in case of an emergency, e.g., if you are unmasked as a fraud and must run for your life or fight a gang of outraged cult members. To help preserve your relative strength, keep your followers on a low protein diet. Very low. This will affect both their muscle mass and brain function.

Delegation

Delegate all undesirable tasks. Learn to extract the most work from your disciples with the least effort. Find reliable people to manage daily operations.

Time Management

Do not waste time on trivial personages within the cult, especially time burglars, who ask annoying questions about the holes in your philosophy. Buy The Cult Leader's Day Planner™ to help schedule only the most crucial meetings (such as with your first disciple and your accountant).

Humility

You must maintain the illusion that you are the meekest, kindest, godliest person in your flock, despite the fact you drive the most expensive car—bought with their money. Some cult members may well be cleaning up your very excrement for you as well. Do not let that trouble you! You deserve it!

Fellowship

Create a sense of fellowship by scheduling small treats as if they are a big deal. Few things can create a sense of community more than gelatin desserts, which are always comforting. Stock up on crackers as well.

Mind Control

Make your followers sleep to the piped-in sounds of your own television infomercials. Controlling your followers' thoughts while they sleep is an important tool in maintaining your position.

Beyond the Seven Habits: How to Establish a Successful Cult

Establishing a successful cult demands tremendous effort by the cult's founder, just as with any successful start-up enterprise. Many people have tried to start their own cults without proper training, often with disastrous results. Such ill-starred attempts are characterized by total disdain for human gullibility and a lack of appreciation for the subtleties required for deception on a mass scale. Human history teaches us the critical role played by dynamic individuals in teaching these false "truths" to millions in order to control their lives and take their money.

Indeed, most people do not believe in specific religious ideas—which when analyzed often lead to hopeless contradiction or confusion. Instead, people believe *in other people* whom they believe have greater powers of understanding than themselves. People depend on the *conviction of others*, and this is precisely what you need to supply.

Conceiving Your Cult

First you must choose your target demographic and formulate the theme of your cult.

Few cult leaders have enough originality to start their own belief-systems totally from scratch. Instead, you will probably have to copy some ideas from established belief-systems, such as the Christian or "countercultural" traditions. But be creative! During this time of idea-formation, it is important to let your ideas flow freely. America is all about diversity, and your freedom of self-expression includes creating a cult that reflects your own sense of style. Never forget that.

2

Consider your own intellectual strengths and religious training. If you frequently attended church during your youth, you should work within that tradition, as it will give you invaluable experiences to draw from. But if you have rarely or never attended church, you should attend a few times, at least to learn just how ecumenically lax on moral issues most religious denominations have become. Alternatively, you should attend some leftist gatherings if you intend on working the countercultural angle, or at least study some Eastern religions as fodder for your new syncretic religion.

Of course, you could also create your cult from your own ideas, but this requires the hard work of writing down your "beliefs" in order to garner publicity. If you are intellectually strong, this approach has some merit. If you word your tract carefully, it will be vague enough to withstand the test of time. Besides, you are the ultimate authority anyway. Many people are drawn to a brand "new" philosophy.

Once you have decided on a tradition to work in, you need to develop your "hook," the unique selling point of your cult compared to your competition (i.e., other cults, organized religion, everything else). This idea should be short, memorable, and non-falsifiable. In the golden years of the 1970s anything with "love" in it was a good bet, such as "Share the Love" or "Love is All," but these are now somewhat hackneyed.

Play to your strengths. If you have a business background, you could build a theme around "the Lord's Blessings" or "Pray for Success." Invoke the time-honored scripture about the Lord repaying you one hundred fold for whatever you give to the Lord. Many people take this literally, and will see your collection plate as an extremely efficient mutual fund. Do not divest them of these notions.

Again, if your strengths are intellectual, you are probably shooting for a disaffected countercultural demographic, which remains a large cluster even to this day. Christianity is usually spurned by this group, so try Buddhism, or some form of mysticism. This is also an ideal group if you want to start a belief-system from scratch. But be sure to include references to literary figures like Blake, Rilke or Allen Ginsburg, or to musicians such as Jim Morrison.

Exercise: Formulate the theme of your cult, paying special attention to your target demographic. If you are working within a conservative Christian tradition, be sure you are ready to field questions about such "Christian" topics such as abortion or gun control. If you are working in a vaguely "leftist" tradition, you could try to dismiss all political questions as pointless, but will have to be well-versed in countercultural claptrap such as the writings of the Beats, Carlos Castaneda, or Fritjof Capra.

Preliminary Cult Leader Training: Joining a Cult

It is absolutely essential that you devote at least three months of your life to your training, without which you are beginning your cult on a shaky foundation.

Let us assume you will be working within the "countercultural" tradition.

After you have formulated the theme of your cult, you must undertake some field research. In other words, you should *join* a cult.

Some would-be cult leaders have skipped this vital step to their own detriment. Joining a cult gives you a view of the inner workings of an existing cult, its leaders, and his or her followers. You can learn much by watching a practicing cult leader in action. If the cult is at all successful, you will see a highly developed theme used to good effect.

I recommend joining a cult near its prime, when it has entered its "isolation phase," in which a self-sufficient compound has already been erected to ensure minimal contact with "outsiders."

Joining a cult has its dangers—you may well end up losing your senses and becoming brainwashed yourself. If this happens, face it: you were obviously not cult leader material anyway. Or perhaps, as has happened, the cult leader identifies you as a mole or a spy. If you suspect that cult members are suspicious of you, you must leave immediately. Your field reconnaissance is a dangerous but necessary part of your training. Other cult leaders are correct in wanting to stamp you out.

After a few weeks or months, it will be time to leave the cult. This may well be the most important lesson, for one day you will need to figure out how to stop people from leaving your own cult. Some underdeveloped cults let people leave at any time, no questions asked. Others may ask for a steep "exit donation" until they can find someone to "replace" you in your demeaning manual labor. There are many policies on this. After your escape, formulate a policy that will work for you.

Creating Your Aura

Creating your aura isn't difficult once you understand your target demographic.

- **Hair**. To lead a countercultural cult, grow your hair long. If working within the more traditional Christian tradition, cut it very short. Or make it big and poofy in the televangelist style, but not long.
- **Eyebrows** are also crucial. If the eyes are the windows to the soul, then the eyebrows are the curtains to the drama raging in your eyes. It is essential to develop absolute control over your eyebrow muscles. Highly developed brow muscles are required for "browbeating" skeptics into submission, or to otherwise mesmerize follows with your "intensity."
- **Physique.** For a countercultural style cult, you should ideally be either very thin (the emaciated wise man) or well-built (physical vitality is an

essential part of convincing others of your own health and dynamism). Even portly individuals can lead cults, but this is usually due to believers unconsciously associating you with the Buddha. You should encourage such comparisons.

- **Speaking**. For a countercultural cult, you should probably adopt a soft, soothing speaking voice, as if you have already discovered the great truths of the beyond. Strident, powerful speaking is reserved for leftist political activists who are angry about things. You are selling peace, tranquility and "dropping out" from the world, not political activism.

- **Infallible Pronouncements.** Once you are established, you will have to adopt an oracle's tone of voice. It is essential for you to develop a high tolerance for contradiction early on. Contradictions may be noted by some of your brighter followers, who must be silenced or removed from the group. Thus, it is important to have ready answers like: "Consistency is the hobgoblin of little minds" (Emerson) or "I contain multitudes" (Whitman)—best said in a bellowing voice. If you're working within the Christian tradition, you can use the ever-handy "The Lord works in mysterious ways" to explain away any contradictions.

First Disciple

Early in your practice, even perhaps before your first public appearance, you will need to discover the one person who believes in you implicitly. This person must be willing to walk through fire for you, and will hopefully be unfazed by the frequent contradictions you will be uttering. Such a person may seem like an unlikely, even ridiculous choice (a former convict, a fallen minister, a recovering drug addict still on the brink), but he or she will prove handy in convincing others you are a worthy cult leader. He or she can also perform countless thankless tasks on your behalf.

Note that it is vital that your first disciple *actually believe in you*. Former cult leaders who have allowed a trusted confidante to play the part of first disciple have usually met with disaster. The cult leader and first disciple were sometimes caught gloating together, often seated before a table loaded with cash. The secret they share is too irresistible. No, the cult leader must walk a solitary path, and trust no one; that is his strength.

It is also dangerous to use your spouse/partner as a first disciple, unless he or she is also a very gullible creature. Note too that if your spouse is the first disciple then you might end up sharing the spotlight, which is not to all cult leaders' tastes.

After one person has been genuinely convinced of your powers, then the precedent has been set. Other people can always point to the first disciple's conviction—and then each other's—as evidence of your authenticity.

The Cult in Embryo

Now that you've completed your training, it's time to get your cult off the ground.

College campuses are excellent places to begin cults, as there are so many young people searching for the answers to life's questions. College students are still at an age when they are open to new ideas—as they must be to join your cult. If your marketing budget is small, you may start with posting flyers in the student union. But be sure to include a picture of yourself on the flyer—not just text. This is a cult after all. This is about you. If you are photographed at an oblique angle sitting insouciantly, students will understand the message that you have new ideas.

During the first meeting, *do not let on* that it is the first meeting. Say that you've just been hanging out in Madison, Wisconsin, or Athens, Ohio, where they loved you. Say that you didn't want to leave, but you were "called" to this town. Don't specify whether it was God or your old college roommate who called you.

This is your big chance, so don't blow it. Hopefully you have carefully planned the format of your cult's "meeting" or "service" or "gathering." Music is essential, but you should get someone else to play guitar or piano for you, even if you can do it yourself. Although singing along is OK during the early days of the cult, eventually you will outgrow the need to lend your own precious voice.

Your "message" will probably be some variation on the theme that "society" has deteriorated, and that only grassroots movements such as your own can recapture authentic spirituality. Organized religion is an obvious and easy target and one of your main competitors—after all, you are not yet organized. Other familiar targets include the government, the media, and big business.

Your cult should provide promising answers to some of life's most vexing questions, including:

- **The Afterlife:** You should absolutely promise one. You lose nothing. It is the ultimate post-dated check.
- **Good vs. Evil:** It's clear who is who here. You and your followers are the elect, the good; the rest of the world is deluded or riddled with evil. But it is wise to blame the evil on the Devil, or someone else similarly unaccountable. The world is misguided, not willfully evil, but you and your group have all the answers.
- **The Meaning of Life:** Clearly the meaning of life is to serve God, or whatever you call your particular absolute end. Earthly considerations (including responsibilities to family, friends, and society) are not so important.

After preparing the soil of your followers' minds by attacking common enemies, you are ready to share your own "testimony." This has got to be

6

good. Your testimony should include such classic themes as abusive parents, broken homes, drug abuse, and your own personal struggles with evil itself. You were a normal person once, too, before your calling. Perhaps you had a mystical experience, after which you understood the interrelatedness of all things, or the cosmic oneness. It is helpful to coin a new phrase here, or else people might question your originality.

Remember that your testimony may be your greatest single asset. It is an enriched version of your life-story. It is vital that it is memorable and easy to summarize. It should be a good *meme*. People with fascinating life-stories have started all successful religions. Learn from them.

Cultivating the Cult

In an age of cynicism, your most difficult task is generating enthusiasm. People must leave your gatherings muttering that you are "amazing" or "incredible." If they do not, then you just may not be cult leader material and should consider finding a less inspiring vocation. You could become a Congressman instead.

Like any good marketing campaign, your cult must focus on certain demographic clusters. Although you may already believe that you are universally charming, in reality you will never appeal to all people.

Be selective. Follow these two cardinal rules:

- Target the vast oceans of gullible people out there. (Don't waste your valuable time on skeptics.)
- Target people with low self-esteem.

Conclusion

Starting a profitable religious cult takes research, field work and preparation. Many would-be cult leaders blithely underestimate the skills and talent required to convince other people that they are the messiah and to swindle them out of their money. Some would-be cult leaders have even become brainwashed themselves or have been exposed and then beaten by an outraged mob of once docile followers.

Still others have made the classic blunder of choosing their spouse or best friend (people who know the would-be cult leader too well to have blind faith in him) to serve as their first disciple.

By following the steps outlined above, and by buying some of our associated products, you too can avoid these traps and establish your own highly profitable religious cult.

A Modest Proposal to Convert Shopping Malls into Prisons

Converting shopping malls into prisons is a cost-effective way to create prison space to house America's growing population of non-violent criminal offenders.

America has an undisputed need for prison space, as we keep more than two million people behind bars. The tendency of courts to coddle prisoners makes the cost of housing criminal offenders mount inexorably.

By a happy coincidence, America's stock of shopping malls is aging ungracefully. Malls built during the shopping mall's gold rush days of the 1970s are now depressing environments, plagued by empty stores and roamed by unkempt hooligans. Efforts to convert these malls into community centers are usually ineffective, and an increasing number of these malls—some less than twenty years old—are being razed because they no longer appear to serve any purpose. This is a tragic fall from the vital civic function they once served.

Why not use these cavernous malls to satisfy our government's need for more prison space? It is not so far-fetched once you consider it. Shopping malls tend to be huge, windowless, concrete structures. They feature adjoining parking lots that provide ample room for recreation yards and for buffers between the prison and nearby suburban populations, who wish to keep these convicts at bay.

Refitting a shopping mall into a prison takes surprisingly little effort. The inmates could be housed in the stores themselves. A former shoe store, for example, can house up to fifty inmates comfortably. All stores are already equipped with a metal gate for their front doors. The gate can be pulled down and locked to keep the prisoners inside. And with some "poetic justice," shoplifters can be confined in the very stores in which they once practiced their craft.

At meal times, prisoners can visit a centrally located food court, where extensive kitchen facilities are already in place.

Malls are already designed to hold people in place for the maximum period of time. Consider the design of the parking lots. Special zoning permissions already allow nearby traffic lights to remain constantly green in order to allow people to enter the mall (or prison), while persistently red lights obstruct the exits. Guard posts erected at these bottlenecks would make escape very difficult.

"It's a Mall World After All"

Although simply using shopping malls as prisons could save taxpayers millions of dollars in new prison construction costs, creative incarceration programs could lead to lower operational costs of running the prisons, as well boost our economy by encouraging prisoners to be full-fledged consumers.

The number of guards needed to man a prison is a decisive factor in its operational costs. However, many studies have shown that if prisoners are suitably occupied, then their idle brains do not hatch plans to escape. As expected, installing televisions in prison cells, especially cable television, has led to such atrophy of mind and spirit among the prisoners that guards were scarcely needed in those prisons. Granting unlimited internet access to prisoners will also render many prisoners sedentary and supine, just as with "couch potatoes" and internet addicts in the general population.

Keep in mind that thousands of inmates are non-violent, and serve time only for such crimes as recreational drug use or political dissent. These non-violent offenders can participate in the pilot program.

Let's call it "It's a Mall World After All." The shops in the new prison malls are reopened, but are staffed entirely by prisoners! Constant video surveillance prevents theft. Video surveillance technology is already in such widespread use in shopping malls that equipment upgrade costs are minimal.

At night prisoners can sleep in the stores in which they work, making sure to first lock themselves in with the metal gates already in place. The stores are open every day from 6:00 a.m. to 10:00 p.m. (until 11:00 p.m. during the week before Christmas), and prisoners are scheduled to work ten hours per day.

For their labors, each prisoner is allotted a $10,000 voucher per year to spend in the shops, where the prices are dramatically inflated to match those found in airports or amusement parks. After their ten-hour day work, they have four hours per day with which to shop. The schedules are arranged so that there are always non-violent offenders shopping.

Remember that states currently spend an average of $40,000 per year to incarcerate one prisoner. Under the "It's a Mall World After All" plan, we estimate a savings of $5,000 dollars per prisoner, even after granting each prisoner an allowance of $10,000.

Here's how:

- a $5,000 per prisoner savings in new prison construction costs;
- a $5,000 per prisoner savings in prison guards. A few machine-gun wielding guards can be placed in skylights and at the mall exits, nearly all of which can be blocked off with giant dumpsters containing the waste generated by the mall prison;
- a $3,000 per prisoner subsidy paid by the merchants, taken from the store's profits;
- a $2,000 per prisoner savings in food costs, as prisoners are required to feed themselves at the food court out of their $10,000 allowance.

Assuming the $40,000 currently being spent to keep an inmate in jail, this would save the government $15,000 per prisoner. The $10,000 allowance given to the prisoners pays for itself through lower costs, and by creating a more robust prison economy.

With 400,000 non-violent offenders behind bars, that's a savings of $2 billion per year. Part of the $2 billion should be earmarked to fight the War on Drugs and put even more non-violent drug offenders into the "It's a Mall World After All" program.

And consider the more meaningful lives the prisoners can lead! After a leisurely morning of shopping or browsing, the inmates could visit the food court for lunch. The lunch served at food courts is perhaps more perilous to their health than the fare served at most prisons. Thus, the prisoners' consumption of cheeseburgers, soda, and sweetened coffee will probably decrease their life-spans in incarceration, leading to further cost savings. But making their own unhealthy dietary choices validates the prisoners' self-esteem, giving them the same illusion of consumer freedom as people outside the prison malls.

After lunch, the shopping continues. Or perhaps the prisoners choose to take in a movie. The inmates could prove a captive audience at the cinemas for Hollywood's latest spectacle, providing important focus group feedback in exchange for free movie passes and popcorn.

Credit card companies will certainly take note of this new demographic cluster with secure incomes and infinite time to shop, and so inundate the prisons with credit card applications, albeit with higher interest rates. They will set up booths to encourage passers-by to sign up—and the credit card companies can easily verify the applicant's address. The existing dental and optical centers in malls could be utilized to service the prisoners.

Note that with $10,000 in hand to spend in a fully stocked shopping mall, prisoners would have little incentive to leave, and so security costs would be streamlined. To prevent any black market from arising and breeding gangs, a few shops would be dedicated to serving the prisoners' needs for such vices as cigarettes and soft drugs. Certainly inmates who have smoked some marijuana, and then ambled into a novelty store will become fixated on the available merchandise, and will lack the motivation or will to attempt escape. Prisoners who develop an entrepreneurial knack could also open a few bordellos, knowing that a steady business is theirs for the asking.

Willing prisoners can even sign-up for the "Shop Until you Drop" plan, whereby they forego their rights to appeal, parole, probation, health care, and counseling, in exchange for an additional credit-line of $5,000 per year.

The prisoners will feel much more a part of normal society, and so will be less vengeful and more easily assimilated if they ever rejoin society at large. From their extensive experience in shopping malls, they will have gained the social skills needed to find a place in society, and perhaps a job as a cashier, unless cashier jobs have all been automated away by that time.

A Modest Proposal to Convert Shopping Malls into Prisons

A chief criticism against this proposal is that life inside the prison walls is so appealing that more people would want to go to prison. After all, it seems little different from the lives of the people on the outside, except that their commute to their deadening wage-slave jobs is much shorter than the commute of wage-slaves still on the outside.

But this is an unconvincing critique of the proposal, as there is little danger that many people would deliberately commit non-violent crimes just to be allowed to live in the prison malls. The $10,000 yearly income is simply too small to satisfy most people's needs for cheaply made consumer products that are often disposed of almost immediately after being purchased. Most people would rather work for more consumer goods, even if it means accruing back-breaking consumer debt as well.

A more convincing argument for this proposal is the profoundly beneficial impact it would have on our economy as a whole. The large and growing prison population, while it currently benefits a few companies with lucrative government contracts, is of little use to the economy at large. By transforming inmates with infinite time on their hands into dedicated shoppers or movie viewers, we can spur our economy into even more furious fits of consumption and growth.

And from that, we all benefit.

Are You an AEIOÜ? Take the Breyers-Devere Probe of Human Worth!

Introduction

Human resource professionals are always demanding more efficient psychological tests for their staffs.

Many human resource departments across the country have replaced the Myers-Briggs test with the more efficient Breyers-Devere Probe of Human Worth.

The Breyers-Devere Probe consists of only fifteen questions. While the Myers-Briggs test captures only four facets of human personality, the Breyers-Devere Probe captures five—and with much greater efficiency!

The five personality types measured by the Probe are:

• Absolutists (A) vs. Relativists (R);
• Egotists (E) vs. Team Players (T);
• Intellectuals (I) vs. Feelers (F);
• Optimists (O) vs. Pessimists (P); and
• Übermensch (Ü) vs. Sheep (S).

The Breyers-Devere Probe of Human Worth

Instructions: For each question, select "I agree" or "I disagree."
Hint: Try to forget that this will be read by your current and all future employers. Most people who take the test are not ultimately terminated as a result.

Questions

1. Absolute right and wrong do not really exist, especially in a corporate context.
   [ ] I agree / [ ] I disagree
2. When working on a team, I congratulate other team members for their nominal contributions to my achievements.
   [ ] I agree / [ ] I disagree
3. Spontaneous weeping during a business meeting is perfectly OK. It's not a sign of psychological weakness, depression or mental illness.
   [ ] I agree / [ ] I disagree
4. This may well be the worst of all possible worlds.
   [ ] I agree / [ ] I disagree
5. Parties can be useful platforms for me to showcase my wit and other talents (even if some people there are consuming alcohol or drugs).
   [ ] I agree / [ ] I disagree

6. I am free to do whatever I want without being punished, unlike previous generations who worried about God watching their every action.

[ ] I agree / [ ] I disagree

7. If I am served unsatisfactory food in a restaurant, I demand that the waiter bring me better food immediately.

[ ] I agree / [ ] I disagree

8. Because I'm such a "people person" I would rather meet a new colleague than think up a great new idea that would advance my career.

[ ] I agree / [ ] I disagree

9. Even on my "good days" it is difficult to fight an implacable sense of doom.

[ ] I agree / [ ] I disagree

10. While dining with others, I have the right to the last piece of any shared foodstuff (e.g., chicken wing, pizza slice, slice of bread or cake).

[ ] I agree / [ ] I disagree

11. If I were trapped with my dog and my best friend without food for more than thirty days, then I would probably end up eating both of them.

[ ] I agree / [ ] I disagree

12. I am far more interesting than the average person.

[ ] I agree / [ ] I disagree

13. I secretly like stupid movies, as long as they make me laugh or cry.

[ ] I agree / [ ] I disagree

14. I still see myself with this company in five years.

[ ] I agree / [ ] I disagree

15. When my boss is unfair to me I sometimes stick up for myself (or have harmless fantasies about his or her death).

[ ] I agree / [ ] I disagree

How to Score the Test

Absolutist/ Relativist	Questions 1, 6, and 11. If you agreed with two or three of these you are a Relativist (R); else an Absolutist (A).
Egotist/ Team Player	Questions 2, 7, and 12. If you agreed to two or three of these you are an Egotist (E); else a Team Player (T).
Intellectual/ Feeler	Questions 3, 8, and 13. If you agreed to two or three of these you are a Feeler (F); else an Intellectual (I).
Optimist/ Pessimist	Questions 4, 9, and 14. If you agreed to two or three of these you are a Pessimist (P); else an Optimist (O).
Übermensch/ Sheep	Questions 5, 10 and 15. If you agreed to two or three of these you are an Übermensch (U); else a Sheep (S).

The Design of the Test

Many questions are designed to evoke feelings of injustice in the subjects, as both agreement and disagreement may sound like admissions of guilt. This is perfectly natural; everyone is guilty of something. People who hesitate to answer the questions may be highly nuanced thinkers, i.e., indecisive sheep (S), and so are clearly unfit for senior management, where rapid decision-making is essential.

Human resources who leave the test blank are officially scored as a RTFPS. This is not a mistake, but part of the test's design. By default the test reflects the personalities of most people, even if they don't take the test. This is not a "value judgment" about the quality of human *life*, a value that we feel is best left to the biogenetic industry or other corporate interests to decide. As human resource professionals, we are concerned mainly with what is becoming known in HR circles as "human worth," i.e., the value of human resources (as opposed to technological ones) within a corporate structure.

Moral Absolutist (A) vs. Moral Relativist (R)

Moral absolutists believe in an absolute moral structure, usually based upon a religion or some long discredited belief-system such as Freudianism and Marxism. They are apt to use phrases such as "It's only right!"

Relativists believe that morals are relative to a situation, and can therefore rarely make expedient business decisions, or even decide where to have dinner.

Egotists (E) vs. Team Players (T)

Egotists perform best in individual endeavors, such as the arts, in which it is imperative that a single individual grasps the whole undertaking. They also relate everything that others say to events in their own lives—no matter how remote the connection.

Team Players function best in a team environment, but they may or not be leaders (see Übermensch). Team Players may be Sheep who hide their mediocrity in the crowd.

Intellectual (I) vs. Feeler (F)

Intellectuals approach life mentally rather than emotionally, but can't even have a coffee with you without telling you about some book you never read.

Feelers respond emotionally and immediately, and do not tend to filter experience through their logical faculties. Feelers want their feelings affirmed, and understood, but rarely analyzed, especially by Intellectuals.

Optimist (O) vs. Pessimist (P)

Optimists believe the universe tends toward progress and usually carry themselves in a happy manner that is especially irksome to Pessimists.

All Pessimists believe that they are realists, and that their individual lives are programmed for defeat, whether by God, the Devil, or perhaps a global conspiracy.

Übermensch/Überfrau (U) vs. Sheep (S)

Übermensch types have overcome self-doubt and always act confidently. They are the team leaders if Team Players, and often are blazingly original minds if Egotists. Masters of themselves, they refuse to be dominated by (or even interested in the lives of) other, less interesting, people.

Sheep, whatever their other qualities, follow the herd, and try to hide their indelible mediocrity by blending in. Sheep who are also Team Players, function well in such a milieu, while Egotistic Sheep always make bleating-like noises about being better than the other sheep—and even being Übermensch material—but they seldom are.

Once you have calculated your proclivities to the five personality polarities, find yourself in the chart below.

The 32 Personality Types and Suggested Vocations

Abs. - Rel.	Ego. - Team.	Int. - Feel.	Opt. - Pess.	Über. - Sheep	Likely Careers for Overachievers/Underachievers of Each Type
A	E	I	O	Ü	Chairman of the Federal Reserve Bank/ Ayn Rand's Butler
A	E	I	O	S	Think-tank Economist/ Pretzel Vendor
A	E	I	P	Ü	Self-Help Charlatan/ Philosopher
A	E	I	P	S	Accountant/ The Unabomber
A	E	F	O	Ü	The Antichrist/ Televangelist
A	E	F	O	S	Hollywood Actor/ Street Hawker
A	E	F	P	Ü	Visionary Madman/ Opera Singer
A	E	F	P	S	Homeopathist / Ball Retriever at Driving-Range

Satires

Abs. - Rel.	Ego. - Team.	Int. - Feel.	Opt. - Pess.	Über. - Sheep	Likely Careers for Overachievers/Underachievers of Each Type
A	T	I	O	Ü	World Leader/ Cheerleader Coach
A	T	I	O	S	Robot's Secretary/ Greeter at Wal-Mart
A	T	I	P	Ü	Cult Leader/ Congressional Representative
A	T	I	P	S	Sociologist/ Person Willing to Do Gross Things for Money
A	T	F	O	Ü	The False Prophet/ Football Coach
A	T	F	O	S	Missionary/ Peace Corps Lifer
A	T	F	P	Ü	Orchestra Conductor/ Traffic Manager
A	T	F	P	S	Secretary of the Interior/ Car Washer
R	E	I	O	Ü	Archbishop/ Investment Banker
R	E	I	O	S	Middle-Manager/ Lighthouse Keeper
R	E	I	P	Ü	Venture Capitalist/ Philosopher
R	E	I	P	S	Film Critic/ Extra in a TV Commercial
R	E	F	O	Ü	Prime Minister/ Occasional Poet
R	E	F	O	S	Starbucks Barista/ Town Crier

Abs. - Rel.	Ego. - Team.	Int. - Feel.	Opt. - Pess.	Über. - Sheep	Likely Careers for Overachievers/Underachievers of Each Type
R	E	F	P	Ü	Prophet of Doom/ Weather Forecaster
R	E	F	P	S	Nurse/ Pantomime
R	T	I	O	Ü	First Lord of the Admiralty/ Hot Dog Vendor
R	T	I	O	S	Spineless "Yes-Man" Executive/ Mortgage Broker
R	T	I	P	Ü	Junk Bond King/ Degenerate Gambler
R	T	I	P	S	Poet/ Typist
R	T	F	O	Ü	Marketing Director/ Copywriter
R	T	F	O	S	Marriage Counselor/ Used Car Salesman
R	T	F	P	Ü	Survivalist Leader Movie Usher
R	T	F	P	S	Assistant Coach Lifer Barmaid

Conclusion

While skeptics (often classic REIPS's) may doubt that the test can accurately gauge personality traits on the basis of a few questions, our studies have shown that the Breyers-Devere Probe is accurate enough to determine the fate and future careers for most human resources.

Much more meaningful data is generated about the subjects from the Breyers-Devere Probe than from old-paradigm personality assessments. Corporate clients can also buy supplemental literature, *A Corporate Guide to the Breyers-Devere Probe of Human Worth*, which suggests further conclusions that can be drawn about each prospective employee who has taken the test. For example, applicants who agree with the statement "Parties can be useful platforms for me to showcase my wit and other talents (even if some people there are consuming alcohol or drugs)" may be Team Players, but should also

17

be red-flagged for alcohol and drug abuse testing. Other respondents who disagree may be AEIPS and so fit our Unabomber profile; their home telephones should be wiretapped forthwith. This allows employers an extra level of analysis in regards to their current and prospective employees.

Although the personality of the human animal remains too difficult to map absolutely, the Breyers-Devere Probe of Human Worth marks an advance in personality metrics for employers. Ultimately, through advances in neuroscience, all human actions will be able to be deterministically anticipated, and verbal diagnostics such as the Breyers-Devere Probe may become obsolete. But until that time, such tests remain an indispensable addition to our understanding of human resources.

The New Dictionary of American Cultural Literacy

(With apologies to Ambrose Bierce, author of The Devil's Dictionary*)*

Christmas

n. December 25th, the holiest day on the American Consumer calendar. Christmas is in actuality two separate holidays, known by the same name.

Christian Christmas purports to celebrate the birth of Jesus Christ, and is characterized by such cultural phenomena as Handel's *Messiah*, *The Nutcracker*, Christmas lights featuring the manger scene in 1st century Bethlehem or the Santa Claus menagerie, and the purchase, wrapping, and unwrapping of countless consumer commodities.

Consumer Christmas purports to celebrate human sentimentality, and is characterized by such cultural phenomena as Handel's *Messiah*, *The Nutcracker*, Christmas lights featuring the manger scene in 1st century Bethlehem or the Santa Claus menagerie, and the purchase, wrapping, and unwrapping of countless consumer commodities.

Although many adults face the impending Christmas Season with dread and nausea, most people agree that the tradition should be continued "for the sake of the children" or, more importantly, for the economy.

Christmas Season, The

n. A period of preparation for, and recovery from, Christmas, lasting in retail stores from late July through early January.

Consumer

n. A carbon-based unit of use and purchasing, formerly known as a "human being" or a "soul." The ruling corporate elite now views most American citizens as "human resources" or "consumers" (ideally both), while others are known by epithets such as "welfare bums," "welfare queens" or "useless eaters."

The "consumer" is the descendant of the "rational man" from classical economics, who was thought to be acting out of "enlightened self-interest" even when engaging in such foolish behavior as purchasing lottery tickets, extended warranties on appliances, or Ouija boards.

Since the demise of participatory democracy "consumer choice" is the vestigial Voice of the People, expressing its will through the purchase of iPads and Toyotas.

Cool

adj. 1. Appealing to the latest style: *Cool jacket, dude!* 2. Non-conformist; indifferent to the latest style: *So she wouldn't wear the school uniform? That's cool!* 3. Of, or describing, a fortuitous development: *Cool!*

Credit Card

n. An ingenious plastic device used during the purchasing process to create the illusion that one is not spending money.

Democrat

n. A member of the Democratic political party, and as such a defender of life and liberty. Their defense of life is seen in their opposition to the death penalty. Their defense of liberty can be seen in their pro-choice stance on abortion. Their main appeal to followers is that they are not Republicans.

Drug War, The

n. A policy of the U.S. Federal Government that serves to increase demand for alcohol, tobacco, firearms, and physician-prescribed mind-altering pharmaceuticals.

History

n. 1. An academic subject, once taught and studied in high schools and universities (replaced by social studies or cultural studies), which was believed to consist solely in the memorization and recitation of dates, none of which were remembered after the examination. 2. A time or thing in the past of little account: *That's ancient history.* Or *You're history!* (used by movie heroes just before killing another character).

Internet, The

n. A collection of electronic pages to which anyone can contribute anything, but from which few will more than skim.

Irony

n. A now common mode of discourse whereby what is said is not what is meant. Once largely confined to literary works, irony is now the dominant mode of discourse in American popular entertainment.

Like

adj. 1. Approximately; almost: *She weighed like 200 pounds.*
adv. 2. *Intensifier.* To almost have acted in a particular fashion: *He, like, inhaled that burrito!* (He ate the burrito quickly.)
v. 1. To say: *He was like, Wow!* (He said "Wow!" or something similar to "Wow!")
2. To be: *And then she was, like, Wow!* (After the event, she was excited.)
One of the most flexible words in contemporary American speech, *like* has largely shed its original California "Valley Girl" associations to become a slang staple, whether as adjective, adverb, verb or interjection. *Like* conveys the speaker's admitted lack of authority about whatever the speaker is saying: e.g., *Are you, like, out of your mind?* This suggests the speaker's surprise about or

even admiration for the listener's behavior, without committing the speaker to an actual expression of conviction or even concern. *Like* invites the listener to stop and behold a picture, and so is often followed by a one beat pause before the picture is inserted: *She was like, totally Lady Gaga!* This beckons the listener to conjure and frame an image of Lady Gaga in a more direct way than *She looks like Lady Gaga!*

Model

n. *archaic*, a fashion model. (See Super Model.)

Product Placement

n. A device used in TV and movies whereby a character holds or displays a consumer product for the benefit of the viewing audience. The product is usually held up in an appealing fashion, and so the actor's former training as a model here proves helpful.

Actors from the product placement school of acting are also encouraged to watch hundreds of hours of the TV game show "The Price is Right," which is the *Urtext* of contemporary product placement strategies—a whole hour filled with advertising disguised as a game show.

Republican

n. A member of the Republican Political Party, and as such a defender of life and liberty. Republicans' defense of life is seen in their opposition to safe, legal abortion, their support of gun ownership, their often rabid belief in state-sanctioned killing ("the death penalty"), and their willingness to leave the poor and homeless to their fate ("compassionate conservatism"). Republicans' defense of liberty can be seen in their wish to eradicate the National Endowment for the Arts, NRP and the ACLU, as well as their support for the long-term incarceration of non-violent drug offenders. Their main appeal to followers is that they are not Democrats.

"Saturday Night of Justice"

The Fox Television network's Saturday night lineup, including "COPS" and other shows that feature police raids on the homes of minority men wearing undershirts and smoking cigarettes.

Sitcom

n. A 22 minute teleplay, featuring a laugh track chorus. Sitcoms (originally "situation comedies") usually feature likeable characters (often played by models), who find themselves involved in problems of daily life (to which the unwashed masses watching sitcoms can relate). The situations are usually exaggerated to ridiculous proportions, showing the sitcom's heavy cultural debt to the farce. Unlike the farce, however, sitcoms are rarely funny or even amusing, but rely on the laugh track chorus, which cues the audience that something amusing is indeed happening even though it is not.

In America, the sitcom has now replaced the novel as the most universal vessel of a shared cultural consciousness. People with varying appetites for reading, can nonetheless refer to the key characters and events of "I Love Lucy," "The Brady Bunch," "Cheers" and "Friends," with certainty of being understood, as past generations once enjoyed when referring to Moses, Odysseus, and Hamlet.

Super Bowl

n. One of the holiest days on the TV calendar. The Super Bowl is ostensibly a football game to determine the winner of the American football championship. Once a football championship, it is now a 10 hour television spectacular, which also unveils the most sophisticated new TV Commercials. "Super Bowl Parties" are held in many American households, whose members have scrupulously avoided their biological families during the recent December holidays of Christmas, Hanukkah, and Kwanzaa, among others.

Super Model

n. An idealized representation of female beauty, designed to breed dissatisfaction in male consumers about their mates and inferiority in female consumers about themselves so that they later consume more products in a futile quest for happiness. Once known as "models," Super Models are powerful figures in popular culture whether as the objects of men's sex fantasies or of women's revenge fantasies.

Surf

v. To move through a collection rapidly enough to avoid enjoyment of any one member of that collection, viz. *Channel-surf, web-surf.*

SUV

n. A four-wheel drive vehicle designed to ensure the safety of its occupants and the death of others whom it encounters. Although marketed as "all-terrain vehicles," Sport Utility Vehicles are usually seen on the decidedly asphalt surfaces of American suburbia. SUV's (sometimes called "Suburban Über-Vehicles") represent a vehicular evolutionary apogee, as best stated in the classic SUV ad: "It's what Darwin would drive."

TMI

n. acronym for "too much information," usually said by the speaker to indicate that someone else has shared information that is too intimate or just gross.

TV Commercial

n. A genre of the teleplay, lasting from 3 to 120 seconds, which attempts to persuade the viewer to buy or consume a cultural commodity, including other television commercials.

TV commercials are such a respected genre that awards are given out for the outstanding work in countless categories of the field.

TV Commercials now largely consist of ironic or hyperbolic statements and images, designed to complement TV viewers on their savvy and skepticism about the TV Commercial genre itself. Viewers are then expected to purchase sponsored products anyway (though the products are often not pictured in the ad) to reward the sponsor for their ironic parable.

Junior Bushleague

Cast of Characters (In Order of Appearance)
King Willie the Slick
Lady Hilarious, Wife of King Willie
Sir Newt Gecko
The Grand Inquisitor
Prince Al the Bore
Junior Bushleague

Once upon a time in the United States of Amnesia lived a king called King Willie the Slick. Now King Willie was a popular king, known throughout the land for his big smile and feathery head of hair. But one day King Willie the Slick was caught smoking a cigar that had been dipped in the sweet nectar of a harmonica flower.

In fact, thousands of harmonica flowers had to be cut to extract the nectar for a single savory cigar. And the good people of Amnesia felt that harmonica flowers ought not to be cut for such a purpose, or, even if they were (for truth be told some of the people themselves smoked such cigars), it should be done in privacy, and certainly not by the King under any circumstances, who probably shouldn't be smoking at all.

Even King Willie's nasty habit of smoking cigars dipped in the sweet sweet nectar of harmonica flowers could probably be forgiven. But when the King was asked by the Lord High Tribunal of Legal Crimes whether he had indeed smoked such a cigar, the King had replied: "No no no. One thousand times no, assuming that 'no' means what is often taken for the word 'no' in our language by those in the know. And even if I did, which I didn't, I didn't inhale with undue intention." The people nodded their heads and were relieved that the king had smoked no such cigar, though verily many of the people themselves smoked cigars dipped in harmonica flowers.

Now it came to pass that The Grand Inquisitor appeared on the scene. He had been hired by Sir Newt Gecko, then the leader of the one of the land's two main theater troupes, The Repulsives. Sir Newt and the Repulsives were still mad that King Willie the Slick had stolen the crown from the former king, King George the Petulant, successor to the greatest king of our age, King Ronald McRegan. So Sir Newt Gecko hired The Grand Inquisitor to snoop around King Willie's house. And indeed, one day The Grand Inquisitor caught the King in the act of smoking an especially juicy harmonica-dipped cigar, which came to be known as The Great Smoking Harmonica Cigar. The Grand Inquisitor then wrote a long pamphlet about the King, called "An Inquiry Into the Frequency, Manner, and Duration of the Smoking of Cigars Perpetuated by King Willie the Slick During His

Reign," which in fact recounted every cigar King Willie had ever smoked, harmonica-dipped or otherwise, even before his marriage.

The Grand Inquisitor insisted his pamphlet was true, and expressed his unseemly desire to display some of the sweet sweet cigars in a public forum, but this was not wished for by the people. Instead, the pamphlet of The Grand Inquisitor was read aloud by the town criers throughout the land. And the land was sad. Indeed, for one year the good people of Amnesia turned away from their own affairs to listen to the town criers speak of the "Harmonica Matter," which many people found so loathsome. The matter remained unsettled until the "Harmonica State of the Union," King Willie's finest hour, when he spoke for hours about matters of state, and spoke not of the Great Smoking Harmonica Cigar that The Grand Inquisitor had found. And the people of Amnesia again loved King Willie.

But Willie was growing old, and the time had come for him to step down. His wife, Lady Hilarious, herself wanted to be queen or even king, and was even ready to become the Duchess of Sodom in the Assembly of Amnesia for a time until the people had forgotten about the Harmonica Matter. Lady Hilarious wanted to rule so badly that she would even pretend to like the Sodomites in order to fulfill her designs. But she herself was not yet ready to be the king or queen.

#

Now long ago, during the founding of Amnesia, the Founding Fathers of the Aristocracy had decided that ruling the land was a dull business and that their time was better spent tending to their fortunes and their lawns. They would hire the duller members of the Barely Rich to rule the land for them. And the Founding Fathers of the Aristocracy were wise, and knew that the people might try to enrich themselves or rule themselves or even revolt if they were not constantly amused. So the Founding Fathers created two great theater troupes for the National Theater known as the Dominoes and the Repulsives, whose lead actors would come from the class of the Barely Rich. Every four years they would audition for the role of "King" while the Aristocracy continued to rape the land and improve their golfing skills.

Domino productions were often morality plays that showed the Scales of Justice tipping toward equality, and carried themes such as that the poor were good or that the rich were bad. The Aristocracy never objected to these themes, because they knew that the good people of Amnesia would believe that in the Dominoes they had a voice, and so would not revolt.

The most famous Domino actors of all time were a family known as the Kayes, who, though descended from a Beantown bootlegger, had been blessed by a platoon of especially gifted hair-stylists. The most famous of the clan was King Jack the Haircut. The Kayes slept with beautiful actresses, though rarely with their beautiful wives, and had not produced a king for some time.

The Repulsives staged morality plays of a more religious kind. The most famous Repulsive play, "Morning in Amnesia," showed the Amnesians dancing around gushing fountains of Black Gold, while the Lord smiled down on all. The Repulsives found the Dominoes repulsive, mainly for failing to worship the flag of Amnesia dramatically enough. Nor did they drive big enough Black Gold Burning Carriages. Nor did they attend the Amnesian Gladiators' shows quite enough. It was clear to the Repulsives that something was fishy about the Dominoes, who didn't seem quite as proud to be Amnesians as the Repulsives felt they ought to be.

But for many years the Repulsives relied on character actors, and could not produce a leading man to match the dashing Kayes and their many imitators, including King Willie the Slick. The Repulsives could muster only uninspiring types, men with "character in their faces" but nowhere else. Actors like Dick Dixon, who hired scribes to record his every utterance, though he seemed only to utter the word "chickenshit" all the day long, in reference to his enemies. Dick Dixon also sweated a lot on stage, and didn't shave every day, and shifted his beady eyes around, and was in general an unsavory character. But he seemed to stand for something until he was finally dethroned for his general unsavoriness.

For years the Repulsives could only produce such character actors, including Gerald Fathomless and Bob Archer Daniel Midland Droll, until the Great King Ronald McRegan took the throne. McRegan, known as The Great Combobulator, was just what the good people of Amnesia had wanted for years. He was a very experienced actor and learned his lines well. He also staged big and heart-warming productions such as "Grenada the Grinch (It Must Be Stopped)" and "1001 Libyan Nights" that made Amnesians proud to be Amnesians again, because of how many non-Amnesians could be killed without Amnesians receiving a scratch. Perhaps most impressively, King Ronald McRegan had built innumerable catapults with which to hurl vats of boiling offal upon the Evil Empire. He also promised to build a big net to catch the Evil Empire's catapult shots. And so the land was at ease until the pesky Dominoes asked whether nets weren't made primarily of holes.

Now that it was time for him to step down, King Willie wanted his adopted son, Prince Al the Bore to succeed him as king. Prince Al was a wizard, but an ugly man, and so King Willie had always cast him only in minor, nonspeaking parts. Al the Bore was indeed learned, but no matter what his part, his reviewers were unanimous: he was "wooden." He actually blended into the stage, and did not please the crowd. Al the Bore felt the audience needed more "serious" productions, but it was not what the people wanted. The good people of Amnesia had loved the Kayes for their costume dramas, and King Ronald McRegan (for his charm) and King Willie the Slick (for his burlesques) and even the otherwise unlovable King George the Petulant (for his special effects extravaganzas, such as "Saving Private Oil").

The producers of soul-searching dramas, such as King Jimmy Peanut or Prince Al the Bore, could rarely hold an audience, and were bad box office for the Dominoes as a whole.

Now the Repulsives were not without eyes, and saw plainly that Prince Al the Bore had not won favor in the eyes of the people. They searched the land for a leading man to vanquish Prince Al. Their last offering, Bob Archer Daniel Midland Droll, had lost the audition to King Willie, and had grown depressed and started taking Priapism-inducing potions. Even the costume department could not hide the lump in his trousers, and his good wife had grown terrified. The Right Honorable Sir Newt Gecko had been forced into hiding after it was revealed that he had been caught *in flagrante delicto* with several loose women who had been paid only to caress his soft round head. The other leaders of the troupe were of the usual weak, character-actor stripe that could never land them the role of king.

But then at last they found Junior Bushleague.

Junior Bushleague was the son of King George the Petulant. Junior had led a wayward life until six years before, when he had become Duke of the Lone Thought State. Junior was rumored to be a good Duke for many reasons. He hung so many prisoners that there was always room in his jails. (He wasn't sure how many he had hung, or who they were, but he was sure they were all guilty.) He also kept the Black Gold flowing toward great and small alike—toward the towns teeming with smoking Steel Carriages, as well as toward the colonies of seals and the schools of fish. Like George the Petulant, Junior Bushleague was sure to make battle with pesky Third World principalities that owned the Black Gold that the Amnesians deserved.

Junior Bushleague had other ways to win the crowd. Like King Ronald McRegan, Junior promised to lower ticket prices to the shows for all people. Al the Bore asked whether the Aristocracy and the Barely Rich weren't getting the biggest discount, to which Junior Bushleague responded that they were paying the most already, and so *deserved* the biggest discount. The people had forgotten that under King Ronald ticket prices were less at the door, but programs and refreshments were so high that the show was interrupted by hungry theater-goers, begging food from the Aristocracy and the Barely Rich. King Ronald had also installed pay toilets in the bathrooms (though not for the Aristocracy, who had private facilities). Whenever the Dominoes complained, the Repulsives kept insisting that the ticket prices were low. The Repulsives told the people that the Dominoes would raise ticket prices, but still charge more for programs and for food.

Bushleague also promised to stage more lavish special effects productions, as his father and King Ronald had done. King Willie had produced only small patriotic numbers that neither generated memorable slogans nor quickened the production of patriotic pins.

Perhaps most importantly, Junior Bushleague vowed to cleanse the throne that King Willie had stained with nectar of the sweet sweet harmonica flowers.

It was difficult for the Amnesians to choose their favorite for the role of king. During the audition, both actors had given powerful performances.

In the end, the Amnesians chose Junior Bushleague. They chose Junior for his boyish charm and his resemblance to Ronald McRegan. And because times were so good, they felt they could afford to punish Prince Al the Bore for thinking he could be King despite being so inhumanly boring. "If only Al the Bore were more like King Willie!" they lamented, having already forgotten about the Harmonica Matter.

So a new Repulsive play opened, with Junior Bushleague in the role of king. Almost as soon as they had chosen him, the Amnesians felt something was wrong. Although he had more personality than Prince Al the Bore, the name "King Junior Bushleague" just didn't sound right in their ears.

"What have we done?" cried the people amongst themselves. "Have we crowned the greatest idiot of them all?"

King Junior Bushleague was lost without his script. He couldn't improvise. He often seemed to act out of character, and to speak as if he were channeling the voices of others. He seemed to forget that his part was that of King of Amnesians. Once on stage, he acted like a mere errand boy.

But the flag was worshipped, and more farms became golf courses, and extravagant special effects productions were staged, to which the Aristocracy was admitted for free. And though the poor were not admitted, the people warmed to their choice soon enough.

"He was our choice," they came to say. "So he cannot be all bad. For we, the good people of Amnesia, have chosen him, King Junior Bushleague, to be our king. And surely we are not fools."

Note: Gore Vidal coined the phrase "United States of Amnesia."

Are You a Conspiracy Theorist? Take the Test!

Are you a conspiracy theorist? Please take this self-test.

If you frequently read internet news, then you may have unwittingly become a "conspiracy theorist."

Test Instructions

Please circle the number of the answer that you feel best answers the question. **Note:** In the interest of national security the right answers are generally not provided.

I. JFK Assassination (1963)

Question: Who killed President John F. Kennedy?
1. The Warren Commission proved that Lee Harvey Oswald was a Lone Nut assassin. Anyone who disagrees is a Lone Nut conspiracy theorist.
2. The Oswald-acted-alone hypothesis leaves some nagging questions. And if Oswald acted alone, then why would there still be classified documents about the assassination even to this day? There should be nothing to hide.
3. Oliver Stone hit the nail on the head with that movie *JFK*. But that movie is so old that I forgot how it ended. I guess I'll watch it again on DVD to find out who really killed JFK.
4. LBJ probably did it with CIA help. Get over it. It happens.
5. The international banking cartel ordered JFK whacked because he was returning the U.S.A. to gold- and silver-backed money. He wanted to replace the fraudulent "Federal Reserve Notes" ("US dollars") that They (the secret cabal) now print at will to control the world's boom/bust economic cycle.

II. Moon landing (1969)

Question: Did the U.S. really land men on the moon in 1969?
1. Of course the U.S. landed men on the moon in 1969. We have all seen the famous Neil Armstrong footage: "One small step for mankind."
2. Well, maybe they touched up the TV footage a bit, and the first-ever moon-based broadcast was amazingly clear, but still, the U.S. landed on the moon.
3. The moon astronauts, Neil Armstrong and Buzz Aldrin, were Freemasons who were in on the plot to make a fake moon landing movie.
4. The famous moon landing footage was just a movie, directed by Stanley Kubrick. Kubrick re-used some of the moon landing sets for his classic *2001: A Space Odyssey* (1969). After all, if America could land on the moon in 1969, then why would NASA have *cancelled* their plans to go back in 2020? Couldn't they have kept *just one* Apollo spacecraft with crude 1960s technology in working order?
5. "That's no moon! It's a space station!" The moon itself is older than the earth and is really a space station built by our intergalactic alien masters as a

29

forward outpost to give us the seasons, put us on monthly work cycles, cause women to have their periods, and control the fate of the world. So it really doesn't matter whether the U.S. landed on the moon in 1969 or not. The aliens were there first.

III. Princess Diana's death (1997)

Question: Princess Diana died because:
1. Diana's driver got drunk and had a car accident.
2. Diana's driver got drunk and had a car accident, but there was a cover-up so that certain unsavory facts about the royal family never came to light.
3. MI6 (British Secret Service) killed Diana as a favor to the royal family. The Queen knew that Diana was pregnant, and feared that her possible marriage to Dodi would make him step-father to the future king.
4. Princess Diana faked her own death in order to escape the limelight of constant paparazzi harassment. She still lives in seclusion somewhere, probably France, but sneaks out occasionally in order to perform good deeds.
5. The Illuminati killed Diana and were even confident enough to amuse themselves with ritualistic symbolism, such as crashing her car into the *thirteenth* pillar in the Pont D'Alma Tunnel in Paris.

IV. U.S. Election Fraud (2000) – Bush vs. Gore

Question: Did Bush steal the 2000 U.S. Presidential election?
1. Certainly not! Bush won, fair and square.
2. It was messy in Florida, but the U.S. Supreme Court ordered the recount in Florida to stop. Justice was served.
3. Bush stole it: Katherine Harris, his Florida campaign manager, gave Florida's electoral votes to Bush under dubious circumstances; his brother, Jeb Bush, suspiciously was governor of Florida; thousands of blacks were illegally disenfranchised; and an independent media recount later concluded that Gore won Florida and thus the general election.
4. Gore was happy to step aside and let Bush be President, as long as he got to be the poster boy for the fraudulent Global Warming movement, and later make billions selling carbon credits on the Chicago Climate Exchange.
5. Bush taking power was planned long before. The Bush Crime Family worked with the Clintons in the 1980s to smuggle cocaine into the country via an Arkansas airport. They just hand the presidency back and forth to each other like a trophy to continue the illusion that the U.S.A. is a democracy. Look out for Jeb Bush or Hillary Clinton to be President in the future; it's all part of the plot.

V. 9/11 Attacks (2001)

Question: What is the best explanation for the terrorist attacks that occurred on September 11, 2001?

1. The Official Story: Everyone knows that Osama bin Laden, from his cave in Afghanistan, orchestrated the nineteen suicidal terrorists to hi-jack four airplanes and slam them into the Twin Towers and the Pentagon.

2. Incompetence: The FAA, the Air Force, and the Bush Administration were all incompetent on 9/11. How could the terrorists hit *three buildings* within a 50 minute time span without encountering any resistance at all from the mighty multi-billion dollar US Air Force? And afterwards nobody got fired, only promoted? Strange.

3. Cover-up: The Bush Administration is guilty of a cover-up. Bush resisted any investigation about 9/11 and finally allowed a barebones 9/11 investigation (with less than 20% of the budget of the investigation into the Monica Lewinsky affair). The FBI fabricated ridiculous evidence, including Mohamed Atta's "lost suitcase" containing a Koran, flight manuals, and his will. Another hijacker's passport was "discovered" unscathed in the burning rubble beneath the twin towers.

4. The Bush Administration knew in advance that the al-Qaeda attacks would take place, but let it happen on purpose to rally America for the never-ending "War on Terror" abroad and to attack Americans' civil liberties at home.

5. Inside job: President George W. Bush, a cleverly disguised genius, was the criminal mastermind whose administration planned and executed the 9/11 attacks. His cabal's motives included personal enrichment via no-bid war contracts and control of the Iraqi oil fields. The Bush Administration was in a unique position to order the "stand down" of the U.S. Air Force. *Q.E.D.*

VI. U.S. Election Fraud (2004) – Bush vs. Kerry

Question: Did Bush steal the 2004 U.S. Presidential election?

1. Certainly not! Bush won, fair and square.

2. It was messy in Ohio, but Kerry didn't contest it and CNN said it was OK. So justice was served.

3. Bush stole it: Ken Blackwell, Bush's campaign manager in Ohio, gave Ohio's electoral votes to Bush under dubious circumstances; votes were counted by Diebold and ES&S systems, which are Republican affiliated companies. Kerry won the exit polls in both Ohio and Florida yet somehow lost both states.

4. Bush winning this election had been planned long before. The Bush Crime Family has worked with Kerry before, such as when the Kerry Commission (1987) white-washed the Iran-Contra investigation, and let Ollie North off the hook. Kerry's conceding the election without a whimper is further proof that the election was only a show for the gullible masses.

5. Bush and Kerry were in the secret society Skull and Bones together at Yale, and so they're probably in the Illuminati together now, and they're probably even related by blood, like nearly all U.S. Presidents really are.

VII. Aliens

Question: Do aliens exist?

1. Nope. No aliens. The universe may be infinite, but all life is here on earth.

2. Yeah, maybe there are aliens. If so, the government hides the evidence from the people.

3. Yes, there are definitely aliens.

4. The U.S. Government maintains underground bases for their secret alien masters, like the bases under the Denver Airport.

5. Yes, there are definitely aliens, and moreover the aliens have disguised themselves as the great royal families, and so have been secretly ruling the earth since the dawn of time.

VIII. Airplane Accidents

Select the best explanation:

1. Airplane accidents just happen. If many famous people have died in them, it's probably just because they fly more often.

2. It is conceivable that some minor airplane accidents have been caused by bad people for political gain. Stuff happens.

3. Paul Wellstone was the only Senator who stood in the way of Bush's repressive domestic agenda (U.S. PATRIOT Act), so they just had to whack him.

4. JFK, Jr. was set to run against either Hillary Clinton for New York Senator, or even against Bush for President, when he suddenly died in a plane crash in August, 1999—so somebody whacked yet another Kennedy.

5. Nearly every high profile crash (Lockerbie, TWA Flight 800) has been a deliberate sabotage or shoot-down for nefarious political purposes.

IX. Free Press or Controlled Media?

Select the best description of the U.S. media today:

1. The United States of America enjoys a free press, an independent objective media featuring robust investigative journalism. The media serves as a viable check on the power of the government.

2. There is occasionally some collusion between the media and the Government, but the media still acts independently.

3. The U.S. media is an effective corporate-government partnership. Five or six corporations control 90% of all media in the U.S.

4. The CIA effectively controls the News, and has at least since the 1950s, when Operation Mockingbird placed CIA operatives or assets into key positions in the media. As former CIA Director William Casey once bragged: "We own everyone of any consequence in the media."

5. Most U.S. media is a CIA production, whether via front companies or direct control of the Hollywood studios and major record labels.

X. President Barack Obama

Question: Who is Barack Obama?

1. Barack Obama is an inspiring Chicago politician, who won the Presidency in 2008 because his message of hope, change and peace resonated with a majority of voters.

2. President Obama has been disappointing. His Goldman Sachs connections, his expansion of the war in Afghanistan and intervention in Libya are unseemly for a Nobel Peace Prize winner and supposed Tribune of the people.

3. Obama was really born in Kenya, as his own grandmother has claimed.

4. Obama is a Communist, who is working to turn America into a communist state. Obamacare is just the beginning! He is secretly a Muslim. And he wants to take my guns away!

5. The international banking cartel has groomed Obama since birth to one day play the role of the first non-white U.S. President. This explains why he was able to go from a mere Illinois state senator to the U.S. Senate and President-elect in only four years' time (November 2004 – November 2008).

XI. Mind Control

Question: Does the government utilize secret mind control techniques?

1. Mind Control? That's just fodder for Hollywood movies and spy novels. Hypnotism is about as far as it goes and the government doesn't hypnotize anyone.

2. A 1970s congressional committee uncovered that the CIA spent tax dollars on mind control programs, such as the infamous MK-Ultra program in the 1950s, but that's all over now, thank goodness.

3. Government mind control is now so refined that even famous stars from the movies and music industries (e.g., Madonna, Lady Gaga) are really just mind-controlled sex slaves, used as pawns by the Illuminati, both to influence society, and also for their own personal, sexual gratification.

4. Somebody, somewhere, could just throw a switch (perhaps affecting cellular phone towers), and we would all be instantly mind-controlled. That's why I usually wear this tin-foil hat.

5. Tin-foil manufacturing companies spread many false conspiracy theories in order to boost their sales of tin-foil to tin-foil hat wearing conspiracy theorists.

XII. Money

Question: Which answer best describes the U.S. Dollar:

1. A dollar is a dollar is a dollar.

2. The Federal Reserve ("the Fed") exercises great control over the money supply, and insiders can take advantage of this. What else is new?

3. The Federal Reserve Bank is not even part of the U.S. Government, but is a privately controlled bank, owned largely by rich families, such as the Rockefellers. That's why it's not listed in the government Blue Pages, but as a private bank (with shareholders).

4. The Fed can create boom/bust cycles at will. Inflation represents the government printing more money and issuing more credit. The elite are moving their money out of the dollar into Swiss Francs, gold, land, and commodities before the worthless dollar heads straight into the toilet.

5. Cash will soon be a thing of the past. In the near future we will all be micro-chipped with our bank account numbers. Then if you try to go to an Occupy demonstration, they will just shut off your bank account and you won't be able to buy food anymore.

XIII. America as Big Brother Society

Question: Is America (becoming) a Big Brother/1984/Orwellian state?

1. Everything is fine. What is the problem? Only hysterical liberals are concerned about civil liberties. They *want* the terrorists to win.

2. Sometimes I wish that airport security wouldn't take such undue pleasure in groping me before I board an airplane.

3. It's a little unsettling that we are now under video surveillance pretty much everywhere we go, including on highways and city streets. But thank goodness Google Earth doesn't take pictures of inside our houses. Yet. But the new drones flying over America are starting to do it. Bummer.

4. Ok, I admit it: pretty much everything we do and buy is tracked, especially on the internet. America is already a Big Brother society in all essentials.

5. The Internet is really just the U.S. Department of Defense's computer network. They're just letting us use it so they can track down the dissidents and later put them in FEMA detention centers.

XIV. In General: What Makes the World Go Round?

Question: Which of the following best describes how the world works?

1. Stuff happens.

2. Money makes the world go round. Thus, rich people have more power to influence events than other people.

3. Nothing really important happens—murder, arson, war—unless somebody somewhere is making money from it.

4. The Super Rich meet to discuss and plan world events, but luckily for the rest of us, internal fighting keeps them from exercising absolute control over the masses.

5. The Super Rich conspire to create a One World Government ruled via multinational corporations with only nominal democratic influence.

XV. One World Government

1. One World Government? That would be great! Then there wouldn't be any more wars and everyone would be equal! It would embody the same fine democratic principles found in the U.S. today.
2. One World Government? The nations of the world will never give up their power to a centralized authority.
3. The United Nations is a stalking horse for One World Government. The plan is to use foreign troops, especially in America, since foreign troops will be happy to fire on American protestors and dissidents.
4. The Illuminati are first planning World War III between America, Russia and China. After that the people will be ready for Global Government.
5. One World Government has been planned by the Ruling Families for centuries; even Nostradamus knew the master schedule and left clues in his work. Technological advances have finally put the dream within their grasp.

Test Results: Am I a Conspiracy Theorist?

For each question, the answer number (the number before the answer) is also the point score (answer #1 is worth 1 point up to answer #5 worth 5 points). Divide by the number of questions (15). This average is your score.

0 to 1.5. Safely in the Mainstream. Whew, you are not a conspiracy theorist. Most likely you just watch Fox News or CNN and still somehow feel you are an informed citizen. If you scored less than 1, then you did not even answer all the questions, showing your utter contempt for conspiracy nonsense.
1.6 to 2.2. You are not a conspiracy theorist! Maybe you have read a few stories from the alternative press. You were briefly outraged by the injustice of it all, but you will live out your days comfortably in the mainstream.
2.3 to 3.2. Borderline case. You have an interest in alternative explanations. You are out of the mainstream, but America is still a free country, right?
3.3 to 4. Conspiracy Theorist! You actual *prefer* a conspiracy theory to other explanations. For you, the mainstream media is basically disinformation. You read way too much internet "news." Try to go outside a little more.
4+. Paranoid Conspiracy Theorist! Bona fide tinfoil hat wearer! You are compulsively attracted to comprehensive conspiracy theories that try to explain the seemingly random violence in the world.

Conclusion

Because world events are chaotic and disturbing, people take comfort in the thought that events are still under control by *someone*, even if by a super-wealthy elite that may even be a front for aliens that want to kill us all.

While we could not always present the *correct* answers to these mysteries of recent history, at least you can now see where you stand on the *psychological* spectrum of conspiracy theorists.

The Pathetic Lives of Satirists and Critics

An Analysis by The Raynd Corporation

It seems that certain treacherous elements within our society continue to criticize the government and even engage in personal attacks on its rulers or wealthier citizens. Truly such classes of people lead pathetic lives and should not be encouraged to thrive in our society.

A recent Raynd Corporation study has shown that these malcontents can be easily divided into two classes of people: social critics and satirists.

Social critics are easily identified by their salient traits. Social critics range from unemployed losers to salaried professionals. Many white-collar social critics are Ph.D. educated, but still manage to earn the lowest salary of all Ph.D. holders, hardly more than homeless people.

Social critics tend to be childless; equally sterile in intellectual production (an average of one book and ten published articles per lifetime); and they often donate much of their pitiful incomes to public television—while still secretly watching Fox Television for "sociological purposes" (i.e., in order to find out how "the common man thinks"). Social critics tend to be condescending, but without good reason.

Satirists, while also poor, devoid of vitality and of natural hair, and equally unfit for human companionship (whether romantic, amicable or parental), are distinguished from the social critics chiefly by their bad complexions. Following a Mr. Jonathan Swift, an obscure 18th century Irishman and apparently a patron-saint of these satirists, satirists suffer from hideous boils on the faces, hands, and hindquarters that render their disposition surly and disagreeable. Because of their daily personal agony, satirists naturally seek to shift the blame for their woes upon others.

Yet since they know few people personally, and are reclusive, satirists are forced to take aim at fictitious targets. In this, satirists seem to follow the low-salaried Mr. Swift. Our researchers discovered an obscure 18th century children's book called *Gulliver's Travels* wherein Mr. Swift seems to be making fun of little people, big people, and horses by giving them all funny names. Surely, satirists are an even lower specimen than social critics, who at least are balanced enough to focus their critiques on actual targets rather than phantoms of their own disturbed psyches.

But we include this brief sketch of the social critic and the satirist only in the interests of scholarship. Such a miniscule proportion of the population actually *are* social critics or satirists, and their cumulative impact on society is so negligible (their readership consists only of each other), and their combined incomes are such a laughable fraction of the GNP (speech therapy for parrots is currently a more lucrative industry than satire and social criticism combined) that we have decided to conflate these two demographic splinter-groups into one group, whom we call **sat-critters** (satirists and critics).

The Sat-Critters' Inexplicable Motives

While investigating sat-critters in their natural habitat, the researcher is usually driven by one question: *why do they do it?* For what motives do people engage in social criticism and satire? Certainly not for money: for no one makes enough money writing satire to pay for postage stamps, let alone to make a profit. Not for love: for sat-critters are known to be a disagreeable lot, driving away even the most steadfast lovers through transparently false and pathetic expressions of their own importance. Certainly not to effect social change: for almost no one reads social criticism or satire.

It is especially disturbing to note the inordinate effort sat-critters expend to inject wittiness or obscure references in their work—humor and references that only make their work even more inaccessible and unenjoyable to all but their fellow social critics, who have also become soft vegetables through years of lying around with the television on.

As an example of satirists' obscurity, consider the phrase: "Satire is lost on knaves and fools." Our researchers were unable to derive definitive conclusions as to the meaning of this utterance, but are certain that its intended audience can only be other sat-critters. Regardless of its meaning, how is such a phrase actually supposed to effect social change, the expressed intention of the sat-critters? "Knaves" is an archaic word, but the fact that satirists claim that satire is "lost" on anyone shows that it is ill-suited to be a mass-market format, and so will be of marginal social impact. So why do they persist in these pathetic forms of social protest?

It is clear that sat-critters are a despised and disheveled lot, most of who would have committed suicide long ago were it not for the delusions of self-importance their criticism and satire brings them. Thus, sat-critters' labors only "benefit" themselves. Yet surely these delusions of grandeur are best nipped in the bud or uprooted. For their own health and sanity, they should cease their fruitless sat-critting forthwith!

Help Is Available

In the interests of helping these downtrodden misfits, the Raynd Corporation has created the Sat-Critter Fellowship. Those interested in applying for the Fellowship should write to us with the subject "I Confess I Am a Sat-Critter. Please Help Me," and write a brief account of how your life went astray.

In an effort to help all sat-critters nationwide, one hundred fellowships will be awarded. Winners will be given unpaid internships at participating Madison Avenue advertising agencies in New York City, where they will be able to channel their mad visions of society into post-ironic advertising parables, thereby helping these ad agencies to capture the coveted age 10-34

37

"alienation" demographic. In this way, the formally deviant sat-critter can contribute something useful to society.

It is clear that our policy is generous, and only in the best interest of the sat-critters themselves. Our society will be improved not only by eliminating this grating voice of dissent, but also by helping these downtrodden souls to prosper within our system.

Imaginary News

Capitology: Fastest Growing Cult in U.S.

NEW YORK—Capitology, founded in 1987 by Anton Leday, is now the fastest growing religion in the U.S., according to Cult Watch, a mainstream Christian publication.

Capitologists worship a divine presence known as "The Market." During Capitology religious services, the "Manager" of the service will frequently intone: "Let The Market Decide," to which the followers reply: "Amen."

Capitologists believe in the sacredness of human trade, and use elaborate, quasi-sexual symbolism to represent economic transactions. The religion's central symbol is of a hand holding a bill of currency—but it is clearly derived from the Hindu lingam, the holy union of male and female genitalia. Capitologists celebrate five holidays, known as Q1 (March 31), Q2 (June 30), Q3 (September 30), Q4 (December 31), and Christmas Eve, the holiest day on the Capitologist calendar.

Capitologists are not tithed, but are encouraged to make an annual donation sometime before the so-called Day of Reckoning (April 15th, the US tax filing deadline), a day marked by weeping, gnashing of teeth, and highly ritualized protestations of poverty.

The number of Capitology followers grew last year from 893 to 5,617—a nearly sevenfold increase. Capitologists recruit most new followers through their high performance MarkCap™ no-load mutual fund, which earned its investors returns of 67.8% in 1999. Capitology's non-profit status was affirmed by the Supreme Court in a landmark 1994 decision, *Bupkiss vs. Pangreve*. (1999)

Man Claims Local Bagel Shop is a "Basic Human Right"

LOGAN, OHIO—Walter Stanton, 37, has sued the city of Logan, Ohio for "failing to provide bagel facilities equal to that of other cities." A man with an unusually strong love of bagels, Stanton has driven 50 miles to Columbus every Saturday morning for the last year in order to secure his desired baker's dozen of spinach-flavored bagels.

Stanton claims he only seeks equality-of-opportunity for purchasing bagels. "Columbus folks have lots of bagel shops. It's a basic human right. Why can't I have a bagel shop?" lamented a distraught Stanton. (1999)

"People from Families" Should Vote Republican

JEFFERSON, VIRGINIA—Herbert Henry, a Republican candidate for the Jefferson, Virginia City Council, delivered a speech to supporters last week in which he declared that "The Democrats don't love your families as much as I do."

"I'm a Republican. Everybody knows that Republicans are more pro-family. We're the pro-family party," Henry told a gathering of 25 loyal supporters.

"Would a Republican abort a child? Would a Republican spare the life of a man who killed *your* child? No way. The Democrats are just a bunch of liberals."

"Families, and people from families, should vote Republican," Henry concluded. (2000)

Man Injures Shoppers Fighting for "Almost Handicapped" Parking Spot

LOUISVILLE, KY—Joseph Boorman, 32, was arrested today for "felonious parking" after an incident in a supermarket parking lot.

According to Boorman's confession, he had only wanted to buy some packaged cakes, but had circled the parking lot five times without finding a "good" spot. Eventually such a spot materialized ("It was almost handicapped, man!" wailed Boorman during his interrogation), but another driver was closer to the desired spot. Boorman jumped his RangeRover over a steel bicycle rack, landing in the parking space, but bounced and broadsided a Volkswagen Jetta parked in the adjacent handicapped spot, injuring four teen-age soccer players inside. There was no damage to the RangeRover.

Following the instructions on his auto insurance card, Boorman vehemently denied his guilt, even though the accident was witnessed by five on-lookers.

Police office Myron Jones stated: "Boorman is very lucky he didn't make somebody disabled fighting for his almost handicapped parking spot." (2000)

Millions March in the *Who Wants to Be a Millionaire?* Man March

WASHINGTON—In an effort to rekindle interest in the "Who Wants to Be a Millionaire?" television show, the ABC television network sponsored the "Who Wants to Be a Millionaire?" Man March last week in Washington, DC.

ABC aired advertisements for several weeks before the event, encouraging "all people who want to be millionaires to join us in Washington for this historic event." The march, held last Sunday, drew an estimated two million people to Washington's National Mall, according to the Nielsen company.

40

Some marchers carried signs reading: "We Want to Be Millionaires Too" and "Equal Millions for All."

After circling the Capitol and the White House, the procession gathered around the Washington Monument, where ABC had constructed a temporary "Who Wants to Be a Millionaire?" set. Although "Millionaire" host Regis Philbin was unable to attend, former television puppet Howdy Doody proved an able stand-in.

As the hours wore on, the audience grew restless that no player had won $1 million. The very last contestant, however, Hans Van Richter of Westchester County, New York, answered a series of unusually easy questions, including "What is the main alcohol mixed into a gin martini?"

As balloons showered down from the Washington Monument, Howdy Doody asked: "How does it feel to be a Millionaire?" Mr. Van Richter confessed he was "already a millionaire." An angry mob charged the Monument, and Mr. Van Richter and Mr. Doody were forced to seek shelter in the world's largest freestanding stone obelisk.

The National Park Service finally dispersed the mob by dropping a shower of Monopoly™ money on Constitution Avenue. (2002)

Bush May Hold Cheney's Hand During 9/11 Testimony

WASHINGTON—9/11 Commission Chair Thomas Kean agreed today that President Bush may hold Vice President Cheney's hand during their joint, off-the-record, not-under-oath testimony to the 9/11 Commission.

Chairman Kean explained the decision: "Did you see President Bush on *Meet the Press* a few months ago? He could hardly speak in complete sentences. We're sure to get more lucid testimony if Vice President Cheney is there to answer the questions. President Bush might pee his pants or choke on a pretzel or something."

"If Bush testified to us under oath on his own authority, the stock markets would crash overnight from instant panic. Instead, Cheney can squeeze the president's hand really hard or stomp on his foot if he says anything too stupid, which is all too likely."

Vice President Cheney likewise praised Kean's decision stating: "It's a great relief that Chairman Kean has given us the green light to say whatever we like to the 9/11 Commission without any legal consequences whatsoever. Trust me: committing perjury is something you only want to do when it's absolutely necessary." (2003)

Cheney Agonizing Whether to Seize Saudi Arabia's Oil Now or Later

WASHINGTON—Vice President Dick Cheney admitted on NBC's "Meet the Press" Sunday that he was now agonizing over whether to invade Saudi Arabia now or in the "short to medium term."

Cheney admitted it was a difficult time to start a Saudi campaign, due to the stiffening guerilla resistance in Iraq, and the worldwide skepticism over the legitimacy of the U.S.'s March 2003 invasion.

"It's never going to be an easy decision," said Cheney. "People don't realize how complicated it is to plan the back-stabbing of a long-term ally, invade them, and seize their natural resources. The logistics involved! All the phone calls you have to make! But the invasion of our former ally Iraq has been a successful pilot project for this. And besides, we only need to take the eastern half of Saudi Arabia. That's where most of the crude is. We can probably let them keep the rest."

"It's like when you play RISK and you get to place a lot of armies. You get one chance to crush your enemies before they attack you. I have a lot of experience in these things. And I have a Master's Degree. I really know what I'm doing."

The Saudi Foreign Minister had no comment about Cheney's statement. (2004)

Palin Addicts Form "Sarah Palin Anonymous"

BOISE, IDAHO—A Boise, Idaho psychologist, John Baker, has turned his group therapy sessions for local middle-aged Republican men into a formal association called "Sarah Palin Anonymous" or SPA.

Baker stated that ever since Palin's meteoric ascent to the Republican Vice Presidential nomination men forty-and-over began reporting disturbing symptoms such as browsing the internet for hours every day looking for photos and information about Palin.

"She's just so damn sexy," says SPA member Jeb Bowman, 51. "I can't stop thinking about her."

SPA members now number 200,000; more than half are women. Women members are likely to see Palin more as a role model or a reflection of themselves rather than as a sex object. But some women members also confessed they were attracted to Palin even though they had never been attracted to women before.

"She's just so damn attractive," said Lorna Walsh, a SPA Founding Member. "And does she speak truth to power? You betcha!" (2008)

US Supreme Court: Tasing Pregnant Women Not "Excessive Force"

SPRINGFIELD—The US Supreme Court ruled 6-to-3 in *Hartman vs. Springfield Police* that use of a Taser by police is not "excessive force" provided that the officer administering the Tasing possesses "a sufficient background in psychology."

Mary Hartman, a mother of three and nine months pregnant at the time, was pulled over for speeding. She allegedly was driving 27 in a 25 mile per hour zone.

Ms. Hartman denied she was speeding, and explained to Springfield Police Officer Harry Bender that she was driving herself to the hospital to give birth to her fourth child. Officer Bender replied that "the law is the law," and asked her to step out of the car.

After Ms. Hartman refused to step out of the car, Officer Bender told Hartman she was "obviously hysterical" and then Tased her repeatedly in full view of her three screaming children sitting in the back seat.

Justice Scalia read the Court's decision that Officer Bender "utilized his educational background" to determine that the Ms. Hartman and was in need of some immediate shock treatment. Scalia praised Bender's "admirable restraint" in Tasing her in the leg rather than in the stomach near her imminently to-be-born baby.

Officer Bender, who received a grade of a C+ in his "Introduction to Psychology" course at Springfield Community College seven years ago, testified that he "thought she was, like, hysterical."

Drawing on the Taser's relationship with electro-shock, an early form of psychological treatment, the Court ruled that administering a Taser shock was a kind of "on-the-spot therapy for out-of-control criminal suspects."

The ruling was lauded by Captain John Smith of Springfield Police. "The Taser is an important weapon in the police officer's toolkit. We are pleased the Court did not take these important psychological tools out of our officers' hands."

Justice John Paul Jones, writing in dissent, found the term "sufficient background in psychology" itself to be "insufficient."

"What does this mean? That they heard of Freud?" (2008)

Americans Protest Public Health Care, Social Security, and Public Water

WASHINGTON—Over one million Americans gathered yesterday in front of the Lincoln Memorial to protest the implementation of public healthcare. Citing variously "creeping socialism," "Obamacare" or "just wanting to keep

Uncle Sam out of my Medicare," the marchers shared a conviction that even the discussion of public healthcare represents a break with America's past.

The protest featured speakers such as Sarah Palin and Rush Limbaugh. Joe the Plumber was "truly disturbed by America's liberals' latest flirtation with Communism." Even his "Canadian friends" were mortified by the prospect of "Obamacare."

Palin promised that the "Republican President that takes power in 2012— whoever that may be—will roll back the sick Socialist thinking taking root, in Blue States especially."

Limbaugh, after repeating his recent calls for abolishing "public transport and public toilets" (almost spitting the word "public"), told the gathered throng that Obama was also hoping to "inflate socialized retirement."

"True Americans will continue to hold themselves up by their bootstraps rather than accept a retirement income dictated by retirement panels here in Washington, DC."

Limbaugh went on to criticize Obama's "diabolical plans" to "socialize water," and to "ram student loans down the throats of our youth" undermining "their choice of credit options."

Various grassroots movements were represented at the protest, voicing their opposition also to government control of the postal service, national defense, and interstate commerce and banking regulation, all of which, spokesmen argued, might be better served by "private initiatives."

"Liberals just don't understand that corporations have always been the true engine of American greatness," Limbaugh boomed during his speech. "Let's face it: America was founded as a corporation, as the Virginia Company, chartered by the King of England. It's un-American to say that public options are superior." (2009)

New Reality TV Show *Foreclosure*

HOLLYWOOD—The NBS network has announced production of a new hour long reality TV Show called *Foreclosure*, which pays real home foreclosure victims to appear on the show.

Executive Producer John Stallman describes *Foreclosure* as "giving middle-class Americans with TV's a chance to see how much they will suffer if they ever even think about stepping off the treadmill."

Critics gave mixed reviews to the new offering. ABS called *Foreclosure* a "sympathetic portrait of the pain now being suffered by Americans who are being foreclosed upon."

FUX news noted that: "Despite the host's superficial sensitivity about the plight of the victims, the *Foreclosure* camera feels voyeuristic as it follows police throwing families out of their homes, heaping their tacky plastic consumer possessions on the lawn."

The first episode followed the Jones' family all the way from the pinnacle of their $750,000 home down to living as homeless people in a tent city just outside Boston.

Despite some superficial sympathy, *Foreclosure* also insinuates that the Joneses overextended themselves financially and thus brought their misery upon themselves.

The *Foreclosure* pilot also featured an episode about the California multi-millionaire, William Carcassone, whose $1.6 million house dropped in value to $950,000. Carcassone just stopped making payments, seeing it as just another bad investment decision. Banks are hesitant to foreclose on millionaires, fearing they have the resources to drag out the foreclosure process. Carcassone is still living in his home.

FUX News summed it up: "Despite the sympathetic music playing in the background whenever foreclosure victims appear on screen, the overall impact of *Foreclosure* is that of the boot of corporatocracy stomping on a human face again and again. The Message? There's not a damn thing you can do about it."

Viewers reported a sick fascination with the show, but found it oddly compelling. "It's like watching a car accident." (2010)

Obama Drops 10,000 Tons of Boots on Libya

LONDON—The English News Service has reported that the US Air Force has dropped 10,000 tons of regulation army boots of all sizes into Libya. Reportedly, the boots were supposed to have been delivered to an anti-Gadhafi base, but were accidentally dropped by a sortie of planes.

The Obama Administration has denied the incident, asserting that: "We have no boots on the ground in Libya. We prefer to kill our enemies from the skies, showing that we are gods just as powerful as Zeus, who hurled thunderbolts down upon his enemies. Like Zeus, we are dispensing divine punishment from beyond our enemy's reach."

Satellite footage has also revealed thousands of sets of footprints that on close inspection could have only been made by regulation US army boots, such as the kind the US accidentally dropped on Libya earlier this week, before the boots' mysterious disappearance.

Still Vice President Biden supported President Obama by insisting "We will never have boots on the ground in Libya. No boots! I promise! Maybe our mercenaries will, but not the US army." (2011)

US Supreme Court Overturns Social Security

WASHINGTON—Citing the recent decision whereby the Supreme Court overturned Obamacare, the Court has now overturned the Social Security Act of 1935 on the same grounds in *Smith vs. U.S.*

The plaintiff, Orange County millionaire, Weston Smith, sued the Federal Government on the grounds that his Social Security payments forced him to purchase a service against his will and so was "tantamount to slavery."

Justice Scalia cited the recent Obamacare decision and concurred: "The Constitution does not grant the Federal Government the power to compel people to save money for their retirements. The people must be trusted to make their own decisions concerning their retirement futures, which they should entrust into the loving hands of Wall Street and the Federal Reserve."

"Those who are not far-sighted enough to save sufficient funds for retirement deserve to die like dogs under our system of government. God bless America!" Scalia concluded. (2012)

US Unemployment Rate Drops to 0%

WASHINGTON—The Bureau of Labor Statistics reported today that the U.S. unemployment rate, which last quarter stood at 8.2%, has dropped to 0%.

The BLS explained that the US labor force has contracted by about 8.2% since last quarter.

"Americans are choosing to spend more time with their families, or watching television, instead of looking for work," explained BLS spokesman Johnny Divideus.

"Many people no longer wish to work. Others just find combing through dumpsters to be a more profitable use of their time."

"Everyone who really wants a job in America now has one," proclaimed President Obama, "including people who are here illegally. Those who don't have a job must not want it badly enough." (2012)

Meat Packer Introduces Pink Slime Classic™

WASHINGTON—The recent public outcry over "pink slime" in ground beef has led to the removal of the controversial food additive from the beef sold in many supermarkets and fast food chains. Some supermarkets have continued to sell beef containing the "pink slime" additive, and it continues to be served in many public schools.

But some consumers have complained that "pink slime free" beef somehow doesn't have the same taste they are used to.

"Beef trimmings exposed to fecal matter and doused in ammonia sounds perfectly fine to me. We've been eating it for years. What is the problem?" asked Manny Pinto, 31, of Fairfax, Virginia.

"The USDA has always asserted that Pink Slime is perfectly safe to eat. Surely, the USDA would never approve a product that could harm the American public. The fact that it's banned in Canada and in the UK and deemed as unfit even as cattle feed—unless doused in ammonia—means

46

nothing to me. Those countries have socialized medicine, so I don't trust them anyway," Pinto concluded.

"This new pink slime free meat is missing a certain pungency, a certain *je ne sais quoi* that normal beef has always had. I wish they just went back to the old meat," lamented Shelly Balls, 21, of Cleveland, Ohio.

Other consumers have been unhappy that the new, "pink slime" free meat is more expensive. "Hamburger meat is much more expensive now, maybe 3% more," complained Joe Scheisskopf, 55, of Jacksonville, Florida. "Maybe the meat packers are just using this media circus about pink slime as an excuse to raise prices."

Omnivore, the US meatpacking giant, announced yesterday the introduction of Pink Slime Classic™, a new line of ground beef targeted at consumers who are already nostalgic for the special ground beef flavor they have been enjoying for years. Using the slogans "Meat is Meat" and "Slime: The Other Pink Meat" Omnivore plans a nationwide campaign to introduce Pink Slime Classic nation-wide.

Omnivore's media campaign will include a tip-of-the-hat to Wendy's classic "Where's the Beef?" campaign (1984), in which the octogenarian actress Sarah Peller looked at a massive hamburger bun with a small beef patty and famously bellowed: "Where's the beef"? In Omnivore's campaign, a Sarah Peller look-alike will perform a similar gesture but will demand "Where's the Pink Slime?" (Wendy's has proudly claimed to have never used pink slime in their burgers.)

A few conspiracy theorists imagine that this strategic re-introduction of pink slime was part of the meatpackers' plans all along.

"It's just like when they came out with New Coke back in the 80's," said Martín Fierro, 38, of Los Angeles. "Nobody liked New Coke. So when they came out with Coke Classic a few months later, everybody was happy again. I bet the Coca Cola company planned it all along. And the meat packers are no different. With Pink Slime Classic, people will eat more meat than ever." (2012)

Man Who Developed Great Abs Says Life Still the Same

CLEVELAND—John Jaker, 45, a local man who has finally developed great abdominal muscles after years of effort, says his life is still the same.

"I can't believe it! I've been trying to get fit my whole life. When I finally got a six pack [six visibly well-defined abdominal muscles] I thought I would have a lot more confidence. I thought I would get a raise at work. I thought that women would be falling all over themselves for me and my steaming hot abs."

"Instead my life is the same. I got the same crappy job. I'm a little more confident. But I'm still not meeting women. Not even on the internet.

Instead, I seem to be attracting a lot of middle-age guys. It's not what I wanted at all!" Jaker lamented.

"At least I was able to put a photo of my own abs on pleasedateme.com, instead of that stock photo of a guy with good abs that I've been using on my profile for years."

"It's like my abs don't even matter except when I'm at the beach. But here in Cleveland, I don't go to the beach much anyway."

"I try to take my shirt off as much as possible in parks and stuff. And some women check me out. But I think the problem is that my face still looks forty-five, so hot women in their twenties don't even give me a second look."

"So I say: Beware of those false claims about abdominal machines and all those exercise gadgets. Their claims are not true! Even while sporting a rock hard set of abs, I am basically lonely and miserable. And now if I don't keep working out an hour per day, I will lose my precious abs!"

Jaker is considering starting a website to further expose the false claims made by manufacturers of abdominal exercise equipment. (2012)

Amsterdam High School Relocates to Save Historic Coffeeshop

AMSTERDAM—A recent Dutch law forbids the operation of any of Amsterdam's world famous cannabis coffeeshops within 300 meters of a school. While many coffeeshops will be forced to close, one Amsterdam principal has responded to the law by announcing that he will be closing his public high school instead.

"While we support the new law's goal in establishing some distance between schools and coffeeshops, we have decided that the coffeeshops are far more important for the future of Amsterdam than the location of our particular school," said Marc van den Rijn, 59, principal of the prestigious Johan Cruyff New Gymnasium in Amsterdam's city center.

"Unfortunately, our building is only 299 meters from the *Holy Amsterdam* coffeeshop, in a small alley just off the Herengracht. They were here first— since 1975—so we will just have to go."

Van den Rijn's primary motivation was to preserve Amsterdam's tourist magnet, the coffeeshops.

"I am afraid that despite our glorious Dutch weather and world-famous Dutch cuisine, such as pickled herring and boiled cabbage, Amsterdam will become only an obscure, second-rate tourist destination if the coffeeshops are ever closed. In their hearts, everybody knows this."

"Without access to semi-legal weed and hash, tourists who can tolerate merciless North Sea winds and incessant rain might prefer to go to Hamburg or Bruges instead. Hamburg has better prostitutes anyway, as everyone knows. And Bruges has more colorful architecture."

"Visiting the Anne Frank house is educational, but not everyone finds it to be a particularly uplifting holiday experience. Some might prefer Iceland. Or even Euro Disney."

"Our school building needs a major renovation anyway, so we are happy to move outside of the city center and start over in a new building, far away from the venerable *Holy Amsterdam* coffeeshop, where I've been buying weekend hash for myself and my wife since 1975. I'll have to cycle into the city center on Friday evening, but it will be worth it. At least *Holy Amsterdam* will be saved," said van den Rijn.

Holy Amsterdam coffeeshop owner Wim Koepoep stated: "We are pleased with Principal van den Rijn's decision. Since the Johan Cruyff Gymnasium is moving out, we are planning to buy the school building and begin a major expansion, including the establishment of a Cannabis College, where students can study the history and science behind this fine plant, also known as hemp."

"If we all went back to making paper from the renewable hemp plant, as in former times, it would no longer be necessary to chop down a single tree to create paper products, including toilet paper and paper napkins. Hemp is also a superior fabric to cotton in most respects, including its positive environmental impact. Hemp can really save the world!"

So far no other Amsterdam principals have announced their intention to close their schools to save local coffeeshops. (2012)

US Replaces Labor Day Holiday with "Capitalist Overlord Day"

WASHINGTON—President Obama today signed an Executive Order abolishing Labor Day as an "outmoded 19th century relic."

"Since the American labor force is now far too fattened-up and complacent to even dream of conducting a General Strike ever again, we feel confident that Labor Day can finally be terminated without any negative consequences for the capitalist class," announced White House spokesperson Jeremy Peck.

"Most Americans don't even know what a General Strike is anymore. We've done a great job."

A survey of 1,000 Americans asking "What is a General Strike?" proved Peck correct. 54% thought a general strike was a "drone attack on evil-doers," 27% thought it was a bowling term, and only 12% knew its correct labor-related meaning. 7% had no idea what it meant.

"Since organized labor has finally been successfully crushed, we find it hypocritical and counter-productive even as propaganda to continue the pretense that organized labor, or labor itself, is actually valued or appreciated in the United States of the 21st century. Capital is clearly more important than labor, as wise economists have long recognized."

Labor Day was originally declared a national holiday by Congress because of the intense pressure caused by the Pullman Strike of 1894, which ended only days before the holiday was declared.

This change will only take effect in 2015. "People who might consider protesting will shrug it off as a problem for the distant future and resume their channel-surfing or web-surfing," stated spokesperson Peck. "So our challenge to the American people is: 'What are you going to do about it?'"

In its place, starting in 2015, the first Monday in September will be declared "Capitalist Overlord Day." The day will be set aside to honor capitalist overlords, some of whom make more money in one hour than common workers make in entire year. Only people with an annual income of at least $700,000 will be granted the day off. Thus, even the President of the United States, who earns only around $500,000 per year, will have to work that day.

"Why should we as a society continue to honor people who have to work an entire year for what other, more talented people can earn in a single hour?" explained spokesperson Peck. "It doesn't make any sense and it's entirely hypocritical. Labor Day is now as obsolete as labor unions themselves. This reform is long overdue."

Capitalist Overlord Day will also mark the official start to the Christmas season, so as to boost retail sales.

Due to an anticipated decline in the consumption of hot dogs—long a Labor Day staple—the Executive Order also grants compensatory payments to major meatpackers to offset their losses in sales of hot dogs.

Republican Presidential Candidate Mitt Romney applauded the abolition of Labor Day and its replacement with Capitalist Overlord Day.

"This is a change that we were considering implementing in our own administration. So we applaud Mr. Obama for signing this Executive Order. Despite his innumerable faults, Mr. Obama at least knows on which side his bread is buttered, even if he's not a capitalist overlord like me."

Thus, many American workers will be granted one less public holiday every year. Reactions were diverse.

"Well, it's not until 2015 anyway. That's a long-time from now," said Buford Wheeler, 65, of Walla Walla, Washington. "I'll be retired anyway. So it's not my problem."

"I work in retail, so I've usually had to work extra hours on Labor Day. At least other people will have to work now too," said Sarah Bryant, 42, of Cleveland, Ohio. "It's fairer this way."

"I'm just hoping they don't take away Christmas next," said Jeremy Zapp, 23, of New York. "They'll probably say it violates the rights of non-Christians and it will be gone too. These are still the good old days."

"Thank God I live in America," said Jeremy Beaverton, 16, of Beaver Falls, "and not one of those European socialist countries." (2012)

Supporters Praise Romney for "Not Being Obama"

WASHINGTON—While it is clear that millions of people support Romney mainly because "he is not Obama," others support Romney because he vows to rollback health care insurance for the uninsured. Some are impressed with his determination to start another Middle Eastern war. But others are hoping he will gamble their Social Security trust fund on derivatives and other financial products in the open market.

"Even people without insurance often support Romney on health care," says Romney supporter Myron Dickson.

"They prefer to nobly sacrifice themselves and their families by foregoing medical treatment for a higher cause, namely in order to defeat the dark shadow of socialized medicine that has descended upon our land because of Obama. Private insurance companies should continue to maximize profits by denying health care to sick people whenever possible. That's what capitalism is all about."

"Romney also promises to attack Iran, and probably other countries where predominantly non-white terrorist people live. He will probably bomb them with drones just as Obama has done, as the world will never rise up in outrage at this. This promise to continue killing people with drones has also inspired millions of voters," says Dickson.

"Of course, these drones will never be used on the American people."

Bill Daniels supports Romney too. "Romney's got the stones to gamble the entire Social Security trust fund on Wall Street. Obama's been happy with my Social Security making 1% on Treasury Bills. I would much rather entrust my retirement to investment banks with close ties to Romney. I'm sure they have my best interests at heart. This way I am sure to have a more comfortable retirement."

"Never before has a candidate been so wooden and uninspiring and relied so heavily upon his constituents' hatred of a sitting President," said Obama supporter Frank Papillon. (2012)

IRS: Frozen Bodies Are Subject to Income Tax

WASHINGTON—A new IRS rule states that cryogenically preserved bodies (frozen in liquid nitrogen) are still subject to US income tax, "because there remains a discrete chance that their lives and incomes can be restored by advances in medical science."

The ruling states that a US taxable person with sufficient means to preserve his body "should not use his or her cryogenically preserved state as an excuse to exempt themselves from their tax obligations."

"Being cryogenically preserved is not an argument for shirking one's US tax obligations," stated IRS spokesman John Sanders. "Most of the 200 people who have been cryogenically preserved since 1967 are high net wealth individuals with sufficient funds to preserve their bodies. They can well afford to pay their fair share of tax on passive income."

Revenue Ruling 2012-55 also allows that the "expenses directly related to the preservation of US taxable persons are deductible up to $100,000 per year, and up to $185,000 for a married couple," provided that they were never divorced, and are cryogenically preserved "within the same facility." 401(K) plans and IRAs can be rolled over indefinitely either to pay for the preservation of the US taxable person's body or to pay the new tax on their still undecomposed body.

The Congressional Budget Office estimates that closing the loophole for cryogenically preserved people could raise more than $200 million in tax revenue per year.

Some observers saw the new rule as taking aim at Walt Disney (1901-1966), widely rumored to have had his body cryogenically preserved upon his death in 1966.

One anonymous IRS spokesman stated that "Walt Disney has failed to file a tax return since 1966. The new IRS ruling clearly specifies that physical death is not necessarily a reason to terminate a US person's tax obligation. With all the back taxes, interest and penalties, most of the Disney corporation could end up in the hands of the IRS."

"Why should Mr. Disney get to enjoy a relaxing retirement in his cryogenic deep-freeze, while other retirees are forced to take jobs to meet their tax obligations?"

A Disney lawyer stated off the record that: "This is totally absurd. Walt Disney was never cryogenically preserved. That is an urban legend."

In an unusual departure from tradition, Revenue Ruling 2012-55 applies *ex post facto* to all cryogenically preserved bodies, some dating back to the late 1960s. IRS Spokesman Sanders explained that the *ex post facto* provision was justified by the US government's dire current accounts deficit.

"Cryogenically preserved US persons enjoy all the specific benefits of US citizenship. Why shouldn't they have to pay their fair share of income taxes?"

The Cryonics Institute of America (CIA) has already filed a case in US Tax Court against the provision that "cryogenically preserved heads" are still subject to tax even in cases where "the body itself has not been frozen for preservation."

CIA spokesman Carl Bland stated: "It's one thing to say that a cryogenically preserved body might one day be restored and be able to pay his fair share of tax, but a head! How is a thawed out head supposed to get a job after being unemployed for decades! And in this difficult job market!"

But the IRS is firm in its insistence that "the cryogenically preserved head might still contain a vast wealth of untapped intellectual capital, which should not escape taxation, just because it was once frozen and is no longer attached to a functioning body."

The IRS also anticipated the international tax aspects, reaffirming that cryogenically frozen bodies and heads of taxable US persons currently frozen outside the United States remained US persons for tax purposes, and thus still had an obligation to file their US 1040 long form, and numerous other forms, depending on their assets.

The IRS also clarified that frozen bodies or heads that renounced their US citizenship would still need to follow the same exit procedure as living US persons.

"If the preserved head or body of a US person renounces its US citizenship, the head or body must continue to file US taxes for a period of ten years before it is finally exempt from its US tax filing obligations."

"Any arguments against this ruling will be deemed frivolous," affirmed IRS spokesman Sanders.

Mr. Disney was unavailable for comment. (2012)

Jesus Look-Alike To Be Crucified for Feeding 5,000 Homeless People

ORLANDO—A Jesus look-alike was arrested today for violating the Orlando city ordinance against feeding homeless people. Jesús Christos, 33, of Kissimmee, is now being held in Orlando City Jail.

Orlando Police said that early yesterday afternoon Christos began speaking to a small group of twelve friends in Lake Eola park. Slowly, a crowd gathered to listen to Christos' message of love, forgiveness and social justice.

The charismatic speaker soon found himself addressing a spontaneous crowd estimated at 5,000 people. Most of them appeared to be poor or homeless people. Many have claimed that Christos healed them of chronic health problems, including irritable bowel syndrome, leprosy, and lupus.

After someone in the crowd shouted out "We're hungry!" Christos reached into a picnic basket containing two loaves of Wonder Bread and a bag of Long John Silver fish filets. Christos instructed his friends to start sharing the food with the crowd.

In what many eyewitnesses described as a "miracle," the bread and fish did not run out, and appeared to feed all 5,000 homeless people to their satisfaction.

"The bread and fish were divine," said one homeless man, belching happily.

Orlando police arrived on the scene shortly thereafter and dispersed the crowd with tear gas. Police then fired multiple Taser guns at Christos, attempting to electroshock him scores of times because "he would not go down," according to one anonymous officer. However, Orlando police eventually managed to hand-cuff, arrest, and thoroughly strip-search Christos.

Many Orlando residents expressed their outrage that Christos had single-handedly attracted a crowd of unwashed homeless to their city park, in flagrant violation of Orlando's anti-homeless feeding legislation.

"Jesus Christ! Who the f-ck does this guy think he is?" said Rufus Jameson, 35, of Sanford. "Does he think he's above the law?"

Pastor Jude Criter of Orlando's Landover Baptist Church also denounced Christos saying: "Who is this man who befouls our fair city with his crazy talk about the poor inheriting the earth? Hippie misfits like this Christos character are exactly what is wrong with America. It is impossible to build a Christian society in America with this hippie scum walking around stirring up class warfare."

Dr. John Hilarious, Chief of Psychiatric Care at Orlando Memorial Hospital, opined that: "This is an increasing phenomenon in modern society, these marginal figures with their 'messiah complexes.' We're only lucky we didn't have some kind of Charles Manson situation on our hands. And the fact that he allegedly practiced medicine without a license is especially disturbing to us. Most of the people in that park did not have health insurance and so are not worth being cured of their diseases."

Federal Stateside Security (SS) spokesman Wilma Manley stated: "Jesús Christos is simply a domestic terrorist. He organized a flash mob and spread his dangerous ideas to dirty people who have rejected our capitalist system by willfully remaining unemployed in this land of opportunity. They have scorned our precious way of life and deserve to live or die outside of the system."

Penalties for feeding the homeless in Orlando range from a fine for a minor infraction all the way to death-by-crucifixion for "flagrant contempt of the law." A prominent Orlando judge has already ruled that Christos' actions in feeding 5,000 people in broad daylight satisfied the "flagrant contempt" standard, and therefore Christos will be crucified within a few days.

Christos' crucifixion is expected to be a national event. The Orlando Chamber of Commerce reports that the area's hotel rooms are already nearly fully booked. For those not lucky enough to attend, all major TV networks have announced they will cover the event live on television.

"Many Americans just want to see this guy get what's coming to him," explained Chamber of Commerce Chairwoman Nancy Bates.

Disney World spokesman Karen Alloway stated: "We want to assure all Americans that Disney World will remain open for business during Christos' execution." (2012)

Lost Geniuses

Max Sazonov: Russia's Greatest Poet?

Since the end of the Cold War, Western researchers have discovered the works of suppressed Eastern European artists, casting light on their rich, underground activity.

Towering over his contemporaries stands Maxim Maximovitch Sazonov, philosopher and poet, whose bleak vision of an absurd world may eventually earn him a posthumous reputation as one of the strongest poets in Russian history.

Sazonov: Early Life

Sazonov's nihilistic vision of the world seems inevitable considering his upbringing. Born in 1930 in Leningrad, Sazonov lived his entire life behind the Soviet bloc. He was a sickly child: small, red-headed, with only one eyebrow—a single crescent of hair running across his forehead. He had few childhood friends and spent most of his time alone in his room with piles of hollowed out apples, a habit which has given rise to wild critical speculation.[1]

Sazonov's father, Maxim Mikhailovich, worked all his days in a rubber band factory in Leningrad, where he earned a pittance even by Soviet standards and was never promoted. Sazonov scholars have since uncovered a supervisor's evaluation of Maxim Mikhailovich's work ethic:

> Maxim Mikhailovich is doubtless the laziest and stupidest human being I have ever encountered. Ever. Just yesterday I asked him to box some rubber bands as they came out of the machine. I went to check on him an hour later and found him snoring, sound asleep with a large mound of bands piling up all around him....
>
> A few weeks ago Maxim was outwitted by "Stinking Lizaveta," our charwoman, who swindled him out of his paycheck by repeatedly beating him at tick-tack-toe, claiming that going first was a disadvantage. Maxim would have been cheated again and again had I not warned him about the scam. To this day he insists he'll beat her "next time."

Sazonov's mother, Anna, had an equally low opinion of her husband, writing in her diary:

> I long for his death with all my heart. When will he die, Lord God?
> I weep and pray for a stray bolt of lightning, an industrial accident,
> an unfortunate fall out the window. *Anything.*[2]

Thus, Maxim Maximovitch Sazonov grew up in miserable circumstances, son to a hapless father, and a probably insane mother whose repeated attempts to kill her husband—through poisoning, shooting, stabbing, hanging, lethal injection, a high cholesterol diet, dipping his cigarettes in kerosene, giving his name to the secret police, and beating him repeatedly

---

[1] Some critics, including leading Sazonov critic Francois Boulanger, have seen Sazonov's rotten apples as cries of the child's fall from Edenic innocence. Others have seen them as early Sazonovian attempts at sculpture. For a less likely interpretation see George Ranke's *Sazonov: Philosopher, Pervert, Poet.*

[2] In light of these longings, it is something of a mystery why Anna married him at all. The most convincing explanation to date is Anna's excessive appetite, which kept many other suitors away. Reputedly she could devour an entire lamb and gallon of coleslaw during a single marathon sitting, washing it down with a quart of potent vodka. Unfortunately her prayers for his death were not answered, as Maxim Mikhailovich outlived her, dying in 1983, some fifteen years after her death.

with blunt objects—surely wrought damage on her young son's developing psyche. His father, however, believed all these incidents were accidents, mere "tricks of Fate" as he called it, and never suspected his wife's intentions.

Maxim Maximovitch, their only son, was soon sent off to school where he proved a very poor student. Early on, when asked to build a house out of toy blocks, he persistently used rubber balls, which would always collapse. Young Sazonov never realized the inadequacy of his building materials. His elementary teachers write consistently of his "stupendous incompetence," "stone-like mind," and "reading comprehension of a rock." He took an interest in athletics, however, playing goalie for the school hockey team; but his merciless teammates convinced him it was a special honor to play without a helmet, and young Maxim would inadvertently block shots with his head, precipitating some cerebral damage that could explain his late poetry.

As a youth he found little comfort at home. His beloved father served as a potato peeler for the Red Army from 1941-45, and Maxim was left to the care of his violent mother. Due to the acute war-time shortages, she fed him only boiled rubber bands and bland tomato sauce, dubbing the meal "pasta rings."[3] His only childhood friend was the deranged Luttwak, who suffocated in a bowl of oatmeal at the Sazonovs' breakfast table at the age of 16.

The young ladies of Leningrad never took to Maxim either, finding his sex appeal "on a par with cow dung," in the words of one classmate. Maxim's high school class voted him "most likely to marry a woman like his mother," but young Sazonov wore the ribbon proudly, unaware of the jaded insult because of his intense fondness for his mother, who always called him "Frederico" for still-mysterious reasons.

By 1948, the Cold War was in full swing, his father was back at the factory, and young Sazonov miraculously graduated from high school, due to what we now know was a typographical error. That Maxim Maximovitch Sazonov, age 18, semi-literate, the butt of his classmates, would become perhaps Russia's greatest poet since Pushkin, is a tribute to the man's unquenchable drive for self-improvement.

Having no marketable skills, Sazonov chose the path of many young Russians by joining the military. Sazonov chose the navy, and was soon stationed at the main Baltic fleet at Kronstadt. Here he was forced to shave his eyebrow and endure rigorous physical training. But it was here, at the age of eighteen, on board the Soviet minesweeper *Squeegee*, that Sazonov started his now famous poetry journal. His first poem dates July 9, 1948, and reads:

> How I hate my life!
> My life is like vomited borscht.
> Even the dogs pity me,

---

[3] This helps explain Sazonov's strange practice, which he maintained until the last days of his life, of gnawing on rubber erasers.

offering me the food
from their bowls
with sorrow in their eyes.

I hang from God, like a yo-yo
without a string;
no no, like a rubber band
that has snapped,
and lost all flavor.
All is pointless, pointless, pointless;
without a point.
I walk alone, I walk alone, I walk alone.
Alone I walk.
I walk alone.

This early, yet astonishing poetic fragment already displays many themes that would preoccupy Sazonov throughout his artistic life: a bitter hatred of life, the precariousness of life (as seen in the yo-yo and rubber band metaphors), a separation from God, and feelings of unquenchable loneliness. Although in English translation Sazonov's expressions of loneliness may seem merely repetitious ("I walk alone, I walk alone, I walk alone"), in the original Russian ("ja edu soum, ja edu soum, ja edu soum") they show the astonishing rhythmic skill that later would characterize his mature poetry.

Unfortunately Sazonov's early naval career was not as auspicious as his poetry. His frustrated captain petitioned the Soviet High Command to create a new lowest rank (*Asvaditchin*), just for Sazonov. He never learned to swim, and was confined below deck where his duties included re-counting the number of rivets in the ship's hull. He appeared on deck only a few times in his tour of duty, always falling into the Baltic—perhaps not accidentally.[4] But this isolation gave Sazonov the time he needed to create his first major poetic masterpiece, *October, 1950*, which surely will earn him a place among the world's great poets.

Early Works

On the surface, *October, 1950*, appears to be a mere collection of journal entries—a recording of the rather boring details of a young, somewhat stupid, Russian sailor's life. Indeed, the first literary scholar to examine Sazonov's papers, Edmund Ain of Cambridge, concluded that *October, 1950*

> is the mere ranting of a lunatic. I would bury it under a large rock
> for a thousand years were it not for its historical value, the light it

---

[4] A former shipmate of Sazonov reported that many of the sailors pushed the young poet into the sea, throwing cement-filled life preservers at him while he frantically struggled to stay afloat. Luckily, he was always caught in the minesweeper's nets and brought on deck.

sheds on the disturbing effects of communism on young Russians during the early Cold War.[5]

Ain, however, soon passed Sazonov's papers on to the renowned literary critic Francois Boulanger, who immediately realized their priceless literary value, and who can be said to have "discovered" Sazonov. Indeed, my own interpretation of Sazonov's work closely follows Boulanger.

Consider the first stanza:

October 1st, 1950
I am given only
stale bread to eat.
My parents have moved,
and left no new address.
Smerdyakov beats me senseless
every day,
and every day I pray,
I pray,
that America will nuke us.

Already, Sazonov's expression of existential *ennui* achieves staggering power. Bread, the very symbol of life, is stale for Sazonov; and later in the poem we find that "stale" is Sazonov's evaluation of all of western civilization as well ("our ship sails west/ and *still* the bread is stale").

When the poet says his parents have moved, he surely intends it as a metaphor for his alienation from traditional Russian values, because as is well known, his parents did not move, but simply refused to answer his increasingly lonely and hysterical letters.

The mention of "Smerdyakov" in line five has puzzled many scholars, because the *Squeegee*'s logs show that no one of that name ever served on board that ship, or indeed in the Soviet navy at all. "Smerdyakov," however, is the name of the fourth son in Dostoevsky's *The Brothers Karamazov*. Indeed, since in the novel Smerdyakov is the son who killed Fyodor Karamazov, we see how Sazonov imagines himself a daily victim of horrible crimes ("Smerdyakov beats me senseless every day").[6]

---

[5] Ain believes it is sheer folly to consider Sazonov's *Journal* to be a series of poems at all! For Ain they are merely "journal entries," elevated to the status of high poetry only through "overweening critical interpretation" of critics such as Boulanger. He even contends that the most plausible explanation for Sazonov's now famous "clipped lines"—what Boulanger has called "the most inventive use of free verse to date"—is Sazonov's practice of writing on a very narrow pocket pad.

[6] A less likely interpretation comes from Edmund Ain. Ain's original interpretation of the Smerdyakov character is simply that one of Sazonov's shipmates, Smerdyakovcosmonautskivitch, who did indeed beat Sazonov often, was simply called "Smerdyakov" for short by his shipmates.

The desperate repetition of Sazonov's "I pray/ I pray", so similar to his other characteristic repetitions, shows Sazonov's belief in the futility of prayer. The fact that he prays for a nuclear holocaust is one of the most memorable expressions of a Freudian death wish in modern literature. Boulanger sees Sazonov's lines as a deliberate echo of T.S. Eliot's famous, albeit less subtle, death wish lines:

> I want to die,
> Kill me, Kill me,
> I wish to die.
> I must have a Freudian death wish.[7]

The second stanza continues Sazonov's expressions of nihilistic, pre-post-modern anomie:

> *October 2nd, 1950*
> Last night
> I poked my head
> out of my porthole
> and duckshit hit me
> in the neck.
> I was mad about it,
> but soon got over it.

Here we see Sazonov's persona's efforts to escape the grueling regimen of military life. A simple desire for a breath of fresh air results in a punitive raid of duck excrement, symbolic of an unfeeling cosmos. There has been much critical debate over why Sazonov chose the line "in the neck". On the surface, it seems like a logical place for the feces to land, considering the situation. But the Russian phrase ("u sheu") is ambiguous, possibly meaning "in the neck", but also meaning "on my collar" or "some yoghurt would be nice." In any event, Sazonov shows his characteristic resiliency. At first he is mad ("I was mad about it") at a world that would soil him merely for sticking his head out of a porthole, but the fact that he soon gets over it ("but soon got over it") shows his forgiveness toward a hostile world, despite all the humiliation he has already endured in his young life.

October, 1950 continues for twenty-nine more stanzas, thirty-one in all, and is too lengthy to receive full critical treatment here.[8]

---

[7] These lines were cut from the "The Wasteland" on the advice of Eliot's editor, Ezra Pound, who found them "liberatingly cheerful when compared to the general tone of your poem." Pound himself, however, later stole them, putting them into his last *Cantos* after first translating them into Classical Sanskrit.

[8] Those seeking a full critical analysis of *October, 1950* should consult Francois Boulanger, *Sazonov: Poet and Prophet*. Skeptical critics should keep in mind Edmund Ain's staggering suggestion that *October, 1950*'s thirty-one stanzas are literally thirty-one journal entries, one for each day of the month.

Later Life and Works of Sazonov

A pivotal event in Sazonov's life occurred in the summer of 1953. On leave in Moscow, he decided to pay his respects by attending Stalin's funeral, dead after nearly thirty years of ruthless tyranny. During the massive state funeral, Sazonov ran into an old classmate of his, Voronsky, who told Sazonov that it was an old Russian custom to shout "Down with Stalin!" (or whomever) as a ruler's body is lowered into the ground.[9] With a clenched fist and tears in his eyes, Sazonov solemnly shouted "Down with Stalin!" He was immediately arrested by the NKVD.

At his trial two years later, Sazonov's crime earned him a life prison sentence, as well as an additional forty-five years for contempt of court, for his "audacity" in claiming that he only intended to wish the dictator a peaceful transition to the afterlife. Voronsky, in attendance, laughed hysterically for the length of the trial, stopping only to pare his fingernails.

Thus, Sazonov was unjustly sentenced to exile in the Siberian industrial city of Irkutsk. Here he is said to have met the famous dissident writer Alexander Solzhenitsyn, spilling soup on him. It was also here that Sazonov met the love of his life, Katherina Ivanova.

Katherina, a beautiful poetess, had been sentenced to life-in-exile back in 1949 for writing the lines "…Marx looked like a cat/ and bathed less…" in her never-produced blank-verse drama *Man of Stench*, which dramatized Marx's London years. To her dying day, Katherina defended *Man of Stench* as an historical epic told from the point of view of a "Trotskyite mouth-piece," a character whose political beliefs never reflected her own.

Maxim and Katherina soon fell in love, and remained married for the duration of their lives. Sazonov describes their historic first meeting in his *Journals*:

> During one of my very first days in Irkutsk, I was trying to chop wood, when a beautiful woman approached me, her blonde hair cascading down over her white ski-suit. Immediately, I dropped the ax on my foot. I said: "Ow! That really hurt!" and she nodded compassionately in agreement. We have been constant companions ever since.

Katherina recorded the incident somewhat differently:

> Before I came to Irkutsk I had been subject to many psychological experiments at the secret KGB laboratory in Minsk. One of the political psychologists was trying to prove that women, if pumped full of drugs and subjected to weeks of sleeplessness and hypnotic suggestion, could find even the most repulsive man wildly

---

[9] Stalin of course was not even to be buried at all, but entombed next to Lenin in the Kremlin.

attractive. Then they sent me to Sazonov.[10] I have to admit that under the circumstances I fell in love....Only now, near the end of my life, do I understand I was just a guinea pig for the Soviet scientists, but what can I say about the man I've spent most of my life with? Well...I guess I can say he's the most pathetic hamster I've ever encountered.

Despite this entry from Katherina's journals, most other evidence suggests they were a happy couple. Certainly Sazonov found inspiration from his new wife, and this is reflected in his later works, which display a newfound optimism.

Sazonov's next masterpiece, *October, 1962*, written at the height of the Cuban missile crisis, shows his bravery in the face of potential nuclear annihilation:

What if they nuke us?
I guess I would die.
And Katherina too.
Oh God, Oh God,
I don't want to die
When Katherina acts so odd.

Here Sazonov shows a life-affirming attitude in the face of nuclear annihilation. He admits the reality of his potential death ("I guess I would die") but shows a newfound concern for others ("And Katherina too"). He also expresses a growing religious yearning ("Oh God, Oh God") which is lacking in his early poetry. By "Katherina acts so odd" Sazonov must be referring to his wife's construction of a guillotine, ostensibly for a never-produced political play she attempted to stage in Siberia.[11] But the couple remained happy, as evidenced by numerous photographs showing Katherina's beaming smile.[12]

Sazonov and Katherina remained in exile until 1985, when the new Secretary General Mikhail Gorbachev released many political prisoners. They soon moved to Moscow, where Katherina took a job in a pharmacy, and Sazonov remained unemployed, despite his desire to work with produce. Oddly enough, he seems to have made no effort to publish his poetry. In his later years Sazonov was the victim of paranoid fears that he was really a moose, and avoided social interaction.

---

[10] This research was later used to help secure mistresses for Secretary General Leonid Brezhnev.

[11] Edmund Ain has proposed the theory that Katherina's guillotine was really intended for Sazonov! See Ain, *op cit.*, pp. 56-67.

[12] Edmund Ain, however, believes that Katherina's "happiness" is attributable to her daily drug use ("enough to fell a rugby team").

In the fall of 1989, at the age of 59, Sazonov noted the revolutionary changes occurring in Eastern Europe and so traveled to Berlin to participate. He was even on hand for the collapse of the Berlin Wall, and managed to secure a fragment for himself as a souvenir. But an elderly woman nearby was jealous, and asked him if he would like to trade it for a "moon rock." Sazonov reportedly said "yes, of course" but she bashed him over the head with it anyway. The woman was taken into custody, the police report noting that the "moon rock" bore "an uncanny resemblance to a brick." Unfortunately for the world of literature, Sazonov never recovered from the blow. He staggered around Berlin for a few hours scribbling "Apples and rubber; that is life's meaning," and died a few paces west of the newly-demolished Berlin Wall.

Katherina, on hearing the news of her husband's death, cried "Yes!" and went on a sex spree, wild enough, in the words of one observer, "to make a porno star blush." Though nearing sixty herself, Katherina had retained her figure and was rumored to have satisfied the entire Moscow 6th battalion.

Sazonov's Legacy

Although critics are still poring over Sazonov's massive notebooks, his place in literary history is assured. His work displays a thoroughly modern temperament, an engagement in existentialist issues and a novel use of free verse. Most importantly, his inventive use of journals-as-poetry says more about the nature of time—a perennial poetic issue—than countless books on the subject. *October, 1950* and *October, 1962* ensure Sazonov a place among the greatest of Russian poets.

We can only hope, as scholars unearth more works of Eastern bloc artists, that more Sazonovs will be discovered.

Dr. Claire Hoyt: "Shrink to the Stars"

Dr. Claire Hoyt, once the world-famous "Shrink to the Stars," died in her Burbank, California home last Friday at the age of 79.

Dr. Hoyt is generally credited with conceiving the "Inner Victim," triggering the rise of the Victim Mentality in late twentieth century American society.

Dr. Hoyt, whose patients included two generations of Hollywood stars spanning from Rock Hudson to David Hasselhoff, began her career as a confirmed Freudian theoretician. She later built a client-base consisting primarily of Hollywood actors, who praised her even after she became a notorious leak to the tabloids, describing in detail the confidential secrets of her famous clients.

Early Years

Ms. Hoyt, born in Boston in 1920, claimed in her *Autobiography* (1985) that she was first drawn to psychoanalysis after meeting Freud himself during a family vacation to Austria in early 1938, just before Hitler's annexation of Austria. (Freud was soon after captured by the Gestapo, and, when forced to inform the international press he had been well-treated, wrote ironically: "I can heartily recommend the Gestapo to anyone.")

According to Hoyt's *Autobiography*, Claire saw "Freud himself" purchasing some cigars from a tobacconist in Vienna. She expressed her admiration to the great man, and her own desire to study psychoanalysis. According to Hoyt, Freud replied: "Young lady, you have the eye of a psychoanalyst. If you persist, there is no limit to what you can accomplish." She told the story of meeting "Freud himself" throughout her adult life, often holding the story in reserve for the times when her more outspoken patients expressed doubts about her effectiveness as a therapist.

Although her parents imbued Claire with an unshakable belief in her intellectual powers, her social graces remained undeveloped. Edgar Vinson, author of the definitive Hoyt biography, *Stains on the Analyst's Couch: The Life of Claire Hoyt*, uncovered no intimate friends in her entire adult life—only professional allies who clung to the comet tail of her rising fame. In many ways, the people closest to Claire were her patients, a relationship in which she held all the cards.

Hoyt was accepted into Radcliffe College in 1940 and majored in psychology. During her graduate years, Hoyt underwent the required analysis by her mentor. While in her own self-evaluation Hoyt described herself as "giving, loving, strong, trustworthy," her aged mentor, Professor Liedemann, described her as

> ...an absolutely selfish monster. If she ever became armed with the authority of an analyst she would utterly victimize her patients with the intensity of her own bottomless insecurities, messianic complexes, and intractable neuroses.

Unfortunately Professor Liedemann died mysteriously during Hoyt's analysis, and most of Liedemann's notes vanished after his death. His replacement, the scrofulous Dr. Trachtenberg (later banned from the American Psychological Association for his relations with a fourteen year old female nymphomania patient) waved Hoyt through toward her doctorate with little resistance.

The Selfish Stage

Despite Liedemann's reservations about her stability, her doctoral dissertation, "Self-Help in an Age of Society" earned her a professorship at UCLA. From her new Los Angeles base, Hoyt began her first major psychological studies, which raised firestorms of controversy even in the East Coast intellectual catchment areas.

Her first seminal work, to which she gave the Whitmanesque title "Analysis of My Self," posited a nebulous "selfish" stage in human development, potentially much more persistent than Freud's stages, indeed perhaps lasting even until death.

The selfish stage—certainly not a sinister development according to Hoyt—is characterized by:

> ...a marked preoccupation with the needs and concerns of the self,
> especially in regards to personal advancement, sexual fulfillment,
> and the belief in one's own intellectual equality or superiority *vis à
> vis* others. (*Analysis of My Self*, 13)

Though other psychologists found this formulation spurious ("When are
we *not* concerned with matters of the self?" asked an incredulous Carl
Rogers), the new, psychologically-sanctioned Self-movement spread by word
of mouth, even outside of academia into Hollywood and the California
hinterland.

Case Studies: Fox Boy and "Tail Envy"

Under the aegis of the UCLA Department of Psychology, Hoyt embarked
upon a brief but fruitful period of research. In an attempt to apply B.F.
Skinner's theory of learned helplessness to human sexuality, Hoyt selected a
test group of healthy, sexually active men from the ages of 25 to 49. She
deprived them of sunlight and showed them pictures of the singer Ethel
Merman for eight hours per day for two weeks. Hoyt discovered that these
men were incapable of achieving erections, some even for two years after the
study. She built upon these early studies, later concurring with B.F. Skinner
that a "learned helplessness" characterized the mammalian kingdom—
"especially the males." Such findings made her a darling of the burgeoning
feminist movement.

She also wrote extensive case studies about her patients, some of whom
became famous. A "Louise" came to Dr. Hoyt, because of her chronic
inability to achieve orgasm, whether through self-manipulation or during
coitus with her husband. After eight months of sessions, Dr. Hoyt diagnosed
her with "suspended hysteria," brought about by her living through "an
abnormally short selfish stage between her anal and oral stages." She had
never learned to mentally focus on her clitoral erogenous zone, and so,
without treatment, was "forever doomed to a pathetic life devoid of sexual
satisfaction." Coincidentally, a nurse friend of "Louise" read the story in the
Journal of the American Psychological Association, and told the real Louise about the
article in passing. Louise recognized herself as the subject of the study, and
later told Hoyt's biographers she was shocked to read herself described in the
article as "obviously untreatable," especially as Hoyt had badgered her to
continue her therapy for seven years at great expense.

Yet many patients found the combination of her affected Bostonian
accent and facility with Freudian terminology a spell-binding combination.
Some patients later told Hoyt's biographer that she had claimed to be related
to the Kennedys, which was manifestly untrue. And no matter how troubled
the patient, his or her first session consisted of listening to Hoyt's fifty minute
monologue about her long and growing list of credentials, articles, and

professional commendations however trifling—and sometimes her Freud story.

Hoyt's sessions were erratic, sometimes characterized by the analyst's garrulousness about her own personal problems. Other times she adopted a Trappist silence. Hoyt enforced the 50 minute hour mercilessly, famously sending away one wailing patient, the actress Natalie Capriotti, who had finally achieved "breakthrough" about the death of her father during her childhood.

Another of her famous studies concerned the "Fox Boy," who suffered from recurring nightmares that he was a fox eating live chickens straight out of the chicken coop. He could no longer tolerate eating chicken or eggs, and suffered from the daytime hallucination that he had a big, bushy tail. Hoyt noted how the boy would lovingly stroke the tail of her cat, Gertrude, during sessions, and from this conceived her celebrated theory of "tail envy."

"Much as amputees experience a strange sensation in the field of their missing limb," wrote Hoyt, "so children feel the absence of their tails, lost in the mist of time to the process of evolution." Hoyt even posited the shocking assertion that Freud was mistaken about girls' experiencing penis envy, and argued that they experience "tail envy" of animals instead. But she never was unable to cure the hapless "Fox Boy," who endured a disturbed adulthood.

"Shrink to the Stars"

Although her published case studies had earned her a degree of respect among professional psychologists, by the mid-1950s Hoyt's clientele consisted of affluent players within the motion picture industry. At about the same time she ceased writing for scholarly publications, but began her weekly column "Clear as Dr. Claire," eventually syndicated nationally.

"Seeing" Dr. Hoyt remained a status symbol for the stars, despite Hoyt's notoriously loose lips. According to the Vinson biography, Jane Fonda recalled eating at Staunton's, then a fashionable Hollywood restaurant, and hearing Dr. Hoyt expounding loudly about Rock Hudson's secret homosexuality to her table of ten during the soup course. Hoyt, to whom Hudson had entrusted with his secret, performed a biting mimicry of his desperate pleas to remain undiscovered, reducing her table to hysteria, according to Fonda. On another occasion Ms. Hoyt disclosed confidential information about Judy Garland's drug-abuse, calling it "weak" of the actress to take drugs for "emotional problems that most teen-agers successfully master." A few stars were appalled by Hoyt's gossiping as a flagrant violation of her profession, and terminated their visits.

Some actors even used Hoyt as a reliable "leak" to the Hollywood tabloids, knowing that if they "confessed" to Dr. Hoyt a vicious libel about a rival, then it was certain to appear in publications such as *The Hollywood Rag*. The actress Elizabeth Clifton confessed to Hoyt her plans to divorce her third husband, who learned she was divorcing him only after reading about it in *Reel to Real* magazine. Actor John Masters successfully exposed his wife's infidelities for divorce purposes by "confessing" to Hoyt the pain she caused him. The news was soon in the tabloids. Masters only had to pay a token alimony, and he later gleefully described his tactic in his *Memoirs*.

Dr. Hoyt's fame subsided in the late 1970s, but was refueled by the publication of her *Autobiography* in 1985, in which she remorselessly described the psychic frailties of her famous patients. David Hasselhoff, for example, had a "Führer Complex" and cried out "But I am the greatest star in the world!" whenever Hoyt pointed out the "little boy within." Hoyt's *Autobiography* dished out so much dirt about powerful Hollywood stars (always through pseudonyms, but it was so easy to decode her) that a backlash was inevitable.

Thus, Edgar Vinson discovered unusually co-operative subjects while performing celebrity interviews for his biography *Stains on the Analyst's Couch: The Life of Claire Hoyt* (1991). Some of the stars were so driven by their vendettas against Hoyt that they were willing to incur damage to their own reputations—by revealing why they were in therapy—in order to uncover the depths of Hoyt's monstrosity. Liza Minnelli, after admitting that Hoyt had diagnosed her with "bottomless narcissism," reported that she received a vehement "You're in denial!" whenever she challenged Hoyt's theory of tail envy, which Hoyt regarded as axiomatic and refused even to discuss.

Cher also reported Hoyt that her accused of denial after she expressed her skepticism that all women since Eve suffered from a "Madonna/Whore" complex. Cher believed she was immune from any Madonna impulses, but asked whether the Madonna/Whore formulation wasn't "just some tight-ass way of saying it's hard to be good." Cher admitted that she only went to Hoyt because it was a status symbol in Hollywood to be analyzed by Hoyt during the peak of Hoyt's reputation in the early 1970s.

Many patients Vinson interviewed described the difficulties they encountered ending their therapy. First, Hoyt would raise her eyebrows archly, "as if the desire to end therapy were itself a new symptom" or "a troubling sign of resistance." Typically, Hoyt would counter by asking the patient how they "felt" about "the idea" of ending their treatment, and would accept only one word "feeling-word" answers to this query. Often these answers would prove unsatisfactory to Hoyt, who would then often recall the patient's deepest wounds, and reduce them to tears by way of diversion.

Patients with more sensitive souls often found it impossible to extricate themselves from Hoyt's care, as interminable sessions were devoted "exploring" how they "felt" about terminating their treatment. Hoyt would exploit these sessions to expose the most unholy recesses of the patient's psyche, yanking the scab off the oldest wounds, necessitating countless additional visits or new prescriptions for many patients.

And yet for the most docile patients, Hoyt assumed an odd laissez-faire policy, as if they were only paying top dollar to speak to a disembodied ear. Shirley MacLaine reported sessions when Hoyt seemed oblivious to what she was confessing, yet would "nod her head in agreement, rhythmically, like those plastic birds that keep lifting their heads to draw water and then dip again." MacLaine even tested Hoyt's level of engagement by spending entire sessions contradicting herself, only to encounter the same metronomic nodding and vapid look of acceptance.

The Inner Victim

Aside from her impact on celebrities, Hoyt's influence will live on through her books. *The Inner Victim* (1978) represented the finale of Hoyt's serious psychological work and was her most influential book. After *The Inner Victim* many people who had never thought of themselves as victims before realized that they too were victims, who had been unwittingly oppressed by society and their parents since birth. Consider:

> We live our lives with the vague sense we have been wronged. Deep down we know we are good and worthy of satisfying lives. We know that we belong. Yet we do not give voice to these thoughts. We know that we have been victimized, perhaps have always been. Yet it is this voice, the voice of the Inner Victim, that will always lead you back to your true self. (*Inner Victim*, 5)

Hoyt had been treating movie stars exclusively for twenty years. Perhaps unconsciously, many of conclusions she reached after years of dealing with pampered stars were now sold to the public at large as if they were definitive assessments of all of human nature.

Building on her work in *The Inner Victim*, Hoyt developed her theory to encompass all forms of human personality. For Hoyt, the fundamental dichotomy in human nature was the "aggressor/victim" (A/V) dichotomy. For Hoyt, aggression took many subtle forms including "strong extroversion, insisting upon the last word," and even taking the last piece of chicken at a barbecue. Victims tend to be passive and weak, but Hoyt insisted that their heightened sensitivity suggested an "artist in larvae," so that her clients tended to be flattered when Hoyt diagnosed them with a "victim's mentality" that "revealed the butterfly within."

The second key to personality for Hoyt was the inner-directed versus outer-directed predispositions. Aggressors could be either. Aggressive, inner-directed people (AIs) tended to destroy themselves primarily and others secondarily. In this class Hoyt placed alcoholics, regardless of the harm they heaped upon others. Aggressive, outer-directed persons (AO)s, tended to have healthy self-esteems, and were content to control others without abusing them. But Hoyt's clients tended to be victim/inner-directed persons (VIPs), often blameless lambs compared to the monsters who had raised or married them.

She encouraged group therapy, trying to cram as many $200-per-hour patients into one room as possible. She even grouped them according to personality type, so that all "inner victims" met together, enduring group sessions of profound silences. The "outer victim" sessions featured heated exchanges, occasionally culminating in violent rows that Hoyt didn't lift a finger to prevent. It was her habit to remain silent as a stone during group sessions, leaving both "inner" and "outer" victims' to their fate.

Hoyt's Legacy

Claire Hoyt left behind an impressive legacy of psychological work, and some would argue an equally vast legacy of psychological wounds. The twentieth century could be called the "Age of Psychology" in that psychological theories widely displaced religious and philosophical explanations of human behavior. Regardless of the quality of her theories, Hoyt helped psychology conquer America and facilitated the spread of psychological jargon. Terms such as "Selfish Stage," "Tail Envy," and "Inner Victim" have entered the language as indispensable concepts to our self-understanding.

Claude Roger: Philosopher or Fraud?

Louis Bloch's critical biography *Claude Roger: Montmartre Mountebank* denounces one of the most influential philosophers of our time as an "audacious plagiarist." Bloch's argument that Roger's books leave an "embarrassing stain" on contemporary philosophy has generated both moral outrage against Roger and a spirited defense of Roger's intellectual legacy—the Post-Linguistic school of philosophy. Devoted students have recently posted the legendary unabridged first editions of Roger's works—which many believe are loaded with plagiarized passages—on the Internet, fuelling debate about whether his originality was really his own.

Roger rocketed to fame at the age of twenty-four during the violent May, 1968 campus convulsions in Paris. As a student protester, Roger quickly published the long manifesto *L'Ordre-Terreur* (*Order Is Terror*), which argued that since the social order in France was enforced by armed police it was *inherently* violent and oppressive.

He wrote: "If France truly believes in democratic principles, it must disband the army and police so that the Will of the people rises to the surface unchecked." Although reviews found *Order Is Terror* "abysmal" and "bereft of scholarship or thought," in the climate of the campus convulsions it earned Roger an assistantship at the Sorbonne, where he has remained on the faculty to this day, despite not having taught a class there since 1987.

Even early in his career Professor Roger focused his energy more on producing works for publication than on teaching. Louis Bloch, a former student of Roger, remembers him holding court with his admirers at a café:

> Monsieur Roger often said things he thought especially witty or insightful. Sometimes he would stop the conversation in mid-sentence, and hold up his hands to silence us while he stopped to write down what he had just said. He believed everything he said had relevance to some book he was writing. As his fame grew, some of us volunteered to serve as his scribes. We learned to watch his face for the discreet nod that meant he had just said something he believed worthy of preservation.

Still there were times when he was forced to take his own notes. Bloch relates one former lover's claim that Roger took notes for his play *La Décapitation et le Capitalisme (Decapitation and Capitalism)* while they made love, scribbling throughout. Today it is not unusual for Roger's dinner guests to see him switch on a pocket tape recorder to record his entire dinner-hour monologue after their small talk has ceased and he has seized the reins of the conversation.

Roger solidified his reputation in 1973 with the publication of *La Littérature et Le Vide (Literature and Vacuum)*, which argued that all writing—from an infant's pre-literate crayoning to *King Lear*—are of "precisely equal value," and that only the dictates of race, class, and gender trick us into valuing so-called "literature" over other forms of writing. But more than a critique of literature, *Literature and Vacuum* set out to show the appalling limits of language itself to represent reality at all. Consider:

> Language always connotes itself self-referentially as a solipsistic *meta-language*, an infinite regress mediated by its own inherent linguistic modality *about* itself, which, *ipso facto*, is incommensurate with "reality" as hitherto described by post-Humean and pre-Heideggarian Western metaphysicians, shackled within the epistemological straightjacket of murky and untestable neo-Kantian *a priori* propositions about our collective ψυχε [psyche].

> Plato's famous condemnation of poetry as dangerous to his Republic sprang from his insight that poetry has the effrontery to claim that it *transcends* language (via metaphor) and so says something "meaningful" about "the world"—rather than just about *other words*, as we now know.

> Science, by atomizing reality into purportedly discrete chunks, makes no such claims of transcendence, but, through its mundane and joyless exactitude, manufactures the pervasive and comforting

illusion that our absurdly arbitrary units of measuring "reality"—the meter, the Celsius degree, the hour, the color "blue"—are worthy nets with which to capture the slippery and incomprehensible *flux*, verb-clusters at best, that "reality" "really" "is." (*Literature and Vacuum*, 514)

Indeed, for Roger, Man's development of language even represents a regression in evolutionary terms:

Because a dog is more in tune with the magical, pre-linguistic world, the dog's barking and growling—indeed, the sounds he emits during defecation—are far more "meaningful" and "poetic" than even the strongest passages in Proust or Dante. (*Literature and Vacuum*, 1056)

A masterpiece of timing, *Literature and Vacuum* was just the book that the generation of philosophers of language weaned on Post-Structuralism had been waiting for.

Roger was quickly heralded as the "Deconstructor-In-Chief" of the Post-Linguistic Movement by Maurice Duchamps, Professor of Non-American Studies at the Sorbonne, who had become Roger's intellectual valet.

Duchamps' seminal work *Uncommunicative Modalities in Roger's Anti-Texts* launched scathing salvos at traditional philosophy, including his famous assertion that "after Roger, those who still study the so-called Great Philosophers sincerely are only like so many naïve children." A flood of articles appeared heralding "The Post-Linguistic Movement," many of which reverentially cited Roger's work as sacred text.

Despite his argument that "the entire linguistic-philosophical enterprise carries no more meaning than a good game of SCRABBLE®," Roger started churning out wordy philosophical tomes at the dizzying pace of four per year for the rest of the 1970s.

Probably the most influential of these, (*Les Mots, Premiers Instruments de l'Oppression Capitaliste*) *Words: First Tools of Capitalistic Oppression* (1976), was an eight-hundred page neo-Marxist interpretation of the Garden of Eden myth from Genesis, chapters 2-3. Roger interprets God as "the Original Capitalist Overlord," who falsely promised Man a labor-free paradise, only to later condemn him to a lifetime of working the soil:

God deliberately places the serpent in Paradise to tempt Adam's new "helpmate" (co-worker), namely Eve, into eating of the Tree of Knowledge (Words), casting Man into the linguistic prison from which he is yet to emerge. Later, when Man unifies to build the Tower of Babel, God senses a threat to his monopoly of ultimate linguistic power. So God confuses Man with a shower of strange tongues, dividing the workers for thousands of years. Capitalists from all ages have found inspiration from this example. (*Words: First Tools of Capitalistic Oppression*, 792)

Despite a chorus of praise for *Words: First Tools of Capitalistic Oppression*, the burgeoning feminist voice in American academia roundly attacked Roger, now a fixture at NYU, for the perceived sexism in the work. They even cited his praise of Adam's idyllic life before the creation of Eve and the expulsion from Eden as an "infantile wish for a world without women."

Painstaking in its linguistic analysis of Genesis (Roger devotes a long chapter to an analysis of the word "fruit"), *Words: First Tools of Capitalistic Oppression* represented perhaps the high-water mark of Rogerian scholarship. Having established his core tenet that "though everything is a text, in the end all texts are meaningless," Roger now turned his attention to analyzing the "meta-meanings" supposedly lurking within otherwise innocent-looking printed words all around us.

Thus, Roger expanded the scope of the Post-Linguistic school by applying its methods beyond philosophy and literary criticism to "cultural artifacts" in our daily lives—letters, postcards, laundry lists, recipes, tax forms, and other "daily contacts with written language." Roger saw a higher social validity to his studies than to traditional scholarship, which concerned itself only with elitist literary and philosophical classics.

Thus, the books of Roger's middle period of 1979-88, such works as *Du Langage Crypté et des Emballages Alimentaires (Cryptography and Food Labeling)*; *Les stratégies du système d'exploitation des Grandes Entreprises (Stratagems of Corporate Enslavement)*; *La Liste comme Archétype (The "List" as Archetype)*; *Les Mots: A quoi a sert? (Words: What Are They Good For?)*; and *Le Calendrier et le Subtexte (Calendar and Subtext)*, represent a neo-Marxian attempt to "bring philosophy to the common man" by analyzing everyday "word encounters."

Stratagems of Corporate Enslavement (1986), critiqued the corporation's growing role in modern life. Roger posited a "Corporate Mother," not unlike Orwell's Big Brother, that will assume many functions of government and the churches. The first essay "The Sticky Note as Ephemeral Text" is typical of Roger's approach. Consider:

> Although regarded by office workers as a harmless, even useful, invention, the Post-It Note (also known as the "Sticky Note" and by other aliases) insidiously undermines the durability of written language. The written word, which in ancient times was etched in stone or painstakingly written with a stylus or feather pen, *stood for* something permanent. Even more than the invention of the microcomputer with its blinking, ephemeral text, the Sticky Note screams the transience of its own message. It also communicates in a blatantly *corporate* manner. When looking at a Sticky Note, we never see the words alone; we see our words in the context of the modern corporate office, always as furthering some task for the Corporate Mother. Many workers now write a significant percentage of their lifetime written output upon this disposable

medium—communicating only with themselves, isolated from their brother workers.

Insidiously, workers come to rely on the Sticky Notes in place of their own, now-atrophied, short-term memories. The Sticky Notes become the very medium of their thoughts, and soon they degenerate into white-collar crime, dropping the desired Sticky Notes into their pockets or purses. Wise companies do not discourage this practice, knowing that even in the home the Sticky Note serves as a silent reminder of the ever-present demands of the worker's corporate life.

Subconsciously guilty for stealing the Sticky Notes, many workers compulsively think about their jobs, or even perform little tasks at home for their Corporate Mother. The Corporate Mother's colonization of workers' homes always begins with the footholds established by pilfered office supplies. The wise corporation even offers to install computers or other expensive equipment in their workers' homes, knowing the salubrious effect this will have on the minds of even the most slothful employees. (*Stratagems of Corporate Enslavement*, 676)

Despite the penetration of some of Roger's analyses, his works grew even denser and more inscrutable than *Literature and Vacuum*—and it is perhaps doubtful that many common men whiled away their free hours reading them. Dr. Nigel Tarreyton of Oxford lamented that Roger, who had once claimed to have deconstructed the validity of both the American Declaration of Independence and U.S. Constitution in twenty-five pages, now "devotes twice that space analyzing a label on a piece of fruit."

He also continued to alienate his feminist critics. His persistent use of the word "Man" for humanity, and his silence on women's issues, had made Roger an enemy of the feminist movement.

Roger's response was his only play, the avant-garde *La Décapitation et le Capitalisme* (*Decapitation and Capitalism*), a pilot for his revolutionary school of theater, "The Theater of Loathing."

First performed in Paris at La Cartoucherie on September 19, 1989, Roger's "spectacle of loathing" depicts a young woman ("The Woman") behind thick dollar-sign ($) shaped steel bars, futilely reaching her hand out of the cage for a crust of bread. The bread, an impossibly large baguette, never fits through the bars despite several hours of on-stage effort by The Woman. The only man in the play ("The Man") wears a black mask, and carries a large club, designed to suggest both the baguette and a phallus. The main action of the play is his repeated urination on the desired bread. Minor variations on this theme occur throughout the play's five acts.

During the final scene, the stage is darkened, and The Man decapitates The Woman with the club: The Woman lets out a long, blood-curdling scream, sustaining it even while a symbolic female mannequin's head rolls up the aisle into the audience. This ending and the play itself received only outraged hisses even from sophisticated Paris audiences.

The five-hour play ran for only two weeks despite lavish financing, and has never been re-produced. Its critical reception was brutal, and even Roger's academic lackeys ran for cover and stayed uncharacteristically mute. Their master had written a disturbingly bad play. Yet Roger remained convinced he had written a masterpiece, and continued to cite *Decapitation and Capitalism* in his own writing as an important work, comparable to the best plays of Beckett, Brecht, or Pinter. Although Roger may have intended *Decapitation and Capitalism* as an olive branch to his feminist critics—as a dramatization of the plight of women in a capitalist society—many people saw it as Roger's greatest chauvinistic outrage to date, albeit a coded one.

Other clouds were gathering around Roger's reputation. By 1992, many American academics were envious of Professor Roger's reputation and feather-light teaching load at NYU, and embarked on an intensive critical analysis of his books. Doubts arose that he alone could have possibly written one million words per year of academic philosophy for the past fifteen years running. Some of his colleagues suspected that most Rogerian research had been conducted by his graduate assistants, or even just spouted off by passers-by in Roger's trans-Atlantic life.

A self-appointed body of fifty professors from the United States, calling itself the Committee against Corruption in Academia (CACA), began to check Roger's footnotes, evaluate his research, and validate the originality of his most obfuscated passages. They also demanded that Roger produce the rough drafts of his works, a request he "wouldn't dignify" by honoring.

After a two-year investigation, CACA met in New York in August 1994 to compile its findings. Rumors circulated that some of Roger's former students had discovered meaningful chunks of their old term papers lurking deep within his mammoth works. One of Roger's former student "scribes," who had once dutifully transcribed his every café utterance, now claimed that long passages of his mumbling had been inserted into the late chapters of his works *verbatim*. Pages of staggeringly Germanic complexity from Hegel, Leibniz, Spengler, and Schopenhauer had also been included, nearly always without attribution.

And Roger's newest *bête noir*, Professor Katelyn Nokin of Michigan State, who had unilaterally spearheaded an independent probe into Roger's personal life, unearthed more than seventy female students with whom Roger reputedly had had sex. Nokin was especially scandalized by Roger's rumored practice of demanding a hot breakfast the morning after a *rendezvous*, and then badgering all of his mistresses (even unlettered prostitutes) to solve ancient philosophical paradoxes that still baffle specialists.

Yet the final report, which was sure to lead to Roger's total disgrace even in France, somehow never appeared. A closed-door session of CACA's central committee unanimously resolved to drop the matter after three days' heated debate. A few committee members later leaked the motivation behind the last-minute silence: Nearly all professional philosophers, in an attempt to sound *au courant* about deconstruction and post-modernism, had been praising Roger in their own publications for years. A full exposé would reveal that most of the fawning professors had scarcely read his works. In the "publish or perish" world of the contemporary university Roger seemed only an extremely effective practitioner of what so many other professors were trying themselves to accomplish.

Roger himself had not been idle during this mortal threat to his reputation. He had busied himself weeding out the most hideous verbal excrescence and shameless piracy from his works, and had already published much slimmer second editions, sometimes at less than half their original length. And the first editions, which were largely unavailable off-campus, began mysteriously disappearing from the shelves of university libraries. Librarians purchased the slimmer, plagiarism-free second editions, effectively concealing the evidence of Roger's scholarly crime from future students. Even more perversely, the first editions became collectors' items, a process that accelerated their disappearance from campus libraries.

Roger became reclusive after his near destruction by CACA. He claimed, in carefully worded answers during a 1996 interview with *Der Spiegel*, that the only accusations that had ever "hurt" him were that his works were "insincere." He claimed to have recently spent four weeks on holiday in the Australian Outback, getting in touch with his inner Man, and developing his "personal primal scream" to "affirm [his] own post-linguistic nature."

Asked about his plagiarism, Roger replied: "Authorship is a bourgeois illusion. No one owns The Words. We all just recombine them." He even claimed that *verbatim* passages of his undergraduates' term papers had been included in his works intentionally in order to bolster his theories of The Death of the Author, and the "inherently communal nature of language."

Roger's Legacy

The sheer size of Roger's collected works makes assessing his legacy problematic. His groundbreaking research into vanity license plates and food labels brought an immediacy and relevancy usually lacking in contemporary philosophy. Works such as *Literature and Vacuum* and *Words: First Tools of Capitalistic Oppression* displayed unprecedented linguistic acuity, even while they paradoxically argued that human language was by now a blunted instrument, less "true" to reality than vibrations emanating from insects or dolphins. Yet the researches of CACA unearthed a hurried and less scholarly Roger, absent-mindedly or otherwise including thousands of words from writers as varied as

Kant and his own undergraduates without proper attribution. The careful scholar must sift through mounds of Roger's lifetime logorrhea in order to find the nuggets of original wisdom lurking within. Yet for these it is perhaps worth the whiff of plagiarism and chauvinism that engulfs them.

Despite the condemnation of Roger's plagiarism, his works have been too influential to perish. *Literature and Vacuum, Words: First Tools of Capitalistic Oppression, Calendar and Subtext* and several other books will be read as long as philosophy is taught in universities. In fact, Roger's first editions are now available on the Internet, and in a recent plagiarism case at the University of Ohio, school officials found that seven students had downloaded Roger's work for inclusion in term papers as their own. So perhaps Roger was right after all: the words return full circle.

Works Cited

Claude Roger: Montmartre Mountebank by Louis Bloch
Order is Terror by Claude Roger
Literature and Vacuum by Claude Roger
Uncommunicative Modalities in Roger's Anti-Texts by Maurice Duchamp
Words: First Tools of Capitalistic Oppression by Claude Roger
Stratagems of Corporate Enslavement by Claude Roger
Decapitation and Capitalism: A Play by Claude Roger

Karl Kinski: "The Anti-Artist"

Works Discussed

Picasso Blockhead
Piece of Shit #2
Rhubarb Pie Gramophone
Straight Red Line on Canvas
Nixon's Mind
Genuine Forgeries
Hair Piece

WASHINGTON, DC—The most comprehensive exhibit ever of the work of "Arbitrary Expressionist" Karl Kinski (1900-75) opened at the Warner Gallery in Washington last Saturday to enormous lines. Some of Kinski's most famous paintings, including *Picasso Blockhead* (1923), *Straight Red Line on*

Canvas (1934), *Nixon's Mind* (1974), and the surrealist film *Rhubarb Pie Gramophone* (1931), were all on display for appreciative art-lovers.

One hundred tickets were given away on a first-come first-serve basis at 8:00 a.m. Saturday morning, but most of these found their way into the hands of venerable members of Washington's panhandler community, who were later seen selling them for more than $200 each to art-hungry fans.

Those lucky enough to gain admittance were privileged to view works spanning Kinski's fifty year career, from *Picasso Blockhead* (1923) (painted before Kinski had changed his name from Jonathan Berkeley) to *Hair Piece* (1975), executed on his very deathbed.

Kinski never fathered his own school of art, but was an artist highly susceptible to artistic fashions, and so his *oeuvre* parallels many developments in twentieth century art, including Cubism, Dadaism, Surrealism, and Abstract Expressionism. Kinski himself later maintained he was always an "Arbitrary Expressionist" regardless of what he painted. But the great critic Jan Kreustadt simply called him "The Anti-Artist, the assassin of all that is sublime."

Picasso Blockhead

Exhibiting *Picasso Blockhead* (1923) alone is a triumph and minor miracle for Warner curator Frank Ballston, as the painting has only been exhibited once before. Although to the untrained eye *Picasso Blockhead* appears to be a mere repetitious box pattern surrounding a crude figure (who can only be identified as Picasso because of the painting's title), many art critics see the repetitious box patterns as precursors to Andy Warhol's *Campbell's Soup Cans* or *Marilyn*. Kinski's work attacks the supposed originality of Picasso's Cubism by surrounding him with mass-produced boxes. Picasso was not amused, and bought the painting anonymously and locked it away, as scholars learned only upon his death and cataloging of his private collection.

Piece of Shit #2

Kinski quickly moved out of his Cubist period, and embraced Dada, especially as practiced by Marcel Duchamp, master of "ready-made" works of art. Kinski was equally intrigued by this playfulness about aesthetic boundaries. He soon created his own infamous *Piece of Shit #2*, a fecal sample of his very own issue, which he instructed gallery personnel to carefully preserve in transparent paraffin wax. *Piece of Shit #2* caused quite a stir during its premiere exhibit at the Hirschire Gallery in Greenwich Village in December, 1927, but has been little seen since. With *Piece of Shit #2*—now presented at the Warner in a hermetically sealed plastic box—Kinski out-Duchamps Duchamp himself as the champion of ready-made art. As Kinski himself reputedly said at the premiere: "I don't know how I do it, I just do it."

Kinski clearly made a strong statement as a ready-made artist, but it is still encouraging to see him grow and embrace surrealism. According to the critic Roger Fry, who will forever be immortalized for coining the term "post-Impressionism" for the period following the Impressionist period, Kinski's surrealism was an advance on Dadaism, in that:

> Kinski's meaningless art was now channeled toward the pro-active *telos* of achieving meaninglessness, whereas in his Dadaist stage his art failed to strive for meaninglessness, even if it achieved meaninglessness inadvertently.

Rhubarb Pie Gramophone

The Warner exhibit even includes a small theater for watching Kinski's 1931 surrealist film *Rhubarb Pie Gramophone*. Borrowing heavily from Buñuel's and Dali's surrealist masterpiece *Un Chien Andalou* (1929), *Rhubarb Pie Gramophone*, despite its lack of sets, script, or actors, was the most expensive American "art film" of its generation. Kinski, who received major backing from Wall Street financiers just before the crash of '29, shot some 45 hours of footage (later reduced to a running time of 5 hours), much of it in his own apartment. Most of the scenes involve the destruction or discoloration of items of Kinski's personal property. Kinski himself appears in nearly every scene in *Rhubarb Pie Gramophone*, mainly performing such bizarre antics as pouring a can of paint over a roast beef, wearing a T-shirt that reads **The System** while sodomizing his girlfriend (a scene he later claimed was a feminist statement on the oppression of women), or reading passages of *King Lear* aloud while a flock of ducks quack in his living room.

The film features a dizzying speed of cuts, and we are shown different images about every five seconds for five solid hours. Kinski once claimed to have dedicated a year of life to editing the film, though Phil Betcher, Kinski's confidante late in life, claimed Kinski once told him he did it in a week.

The title refers to the one recurring image, that of a pie spinning around on a gramophone. As the film progresses we see shots of Kinski trying to cut a piece of the pie as it spins, and butchering it hopelessly, scattering pie filling all over the room. This shot is relentlessly repeated as if it might unlock the key of meaning of *Rhubarb Pie Gramophone*—and many critics have hazarded theories—but in the end, Kinski's film must be taken as his manifesto for the "arbitrary expressionism" that was his answer to surrealism.

It certainly provoked the surrealists. Surrealists such as Buñuel and Dali, and the semi-retired Duchamp attacked Kinski variously for copying their work, diluting the Surrealist cause, and simply for being a bad artist. Kinski usually averred that he was the original, and that other surrealist artists stole his ideas, though most art historians do not endorse Kinski's view.

Although, originally released as a five hour film, the Warner's curators are showing only a fifteen minute selection from *Rhubarb Pie Gramophone*, taken at random.

Straight Red Line on Canvas

Kinski was always ready to adapt to the latest trends, and his *Straight Red Line on Canvas* (1934) shows his early adoption of minimalist techniques. Kinski described his artistic strategy:

> The viewer finds himself immediately transfixed by the red line. It is, indeed, very red, especially in contrast to the stark white canvas. Red and white. Much is explained by this. The clash of opposites: perhaps reminding us of the struggle of the Red and White Russians during the Russian Civil War or the War of the Roses in Henry VII's time.
>
> Even without recourse to history, one is struck by my audacity in presenting a canvas that makes no claims of representing mere objects in nature or reality. Instead, we are presented with an idea—the *idea* of red, and of white. And the line, the red line, is not so much a mere line, as it is a "zip" into our consciousness. We are struck by the red line, much as we are struck by our first meeting with a new person. In that first instant we know more about people, on an intuitive level, than we ever will. Later we will be told their lies, their own version of themselves, and we shall never see them so clearly again. It is the same with my "zip"; we are presented with red in starkest, truest form, before it will begin to lie to us, as red always does. (*Diaries of Karl Kinski*, 564)

Straight Red Line on Canvas (1934), Dan Loathitz Collection, the Art Institute of Weehawken.

Nixon's Mind

Although Kinski had a very successful run from the 1923 through 1934, the onset of the Great Depression lessened demand for his experimental art. He continued to produce paintings in many different modes, even trying the "action paintings" of Jackson Pollack (though Kinski applied paint with a customized slingshot). But Kinski spent decades in the artistic wilderness.

Kinski wasn't to achieve another success for forty years, when his "Oblique" series of painting exhibited in Greenwich Village in 1974.

Nixon's Mind (1974), an enormous and almost totally blank canvas, wasn't intended to be the highlight of the "Oblique" Exhibit of 1974. Kinski later admitted that it took him little time to conceive and execute this work. But for exhibit-goers during the climax of the Watergate scandal, the canvas struck a nerve, and a crowd gathered round the massive work.

The pressing question was whether there was any paint at all on the canvas. Kinski's caption claimed that "the gray speck in the upper right corner suggests the impotence of the mind when facing the great white universe," but few could even make out this gray speck.

The painting may have been forgotten had not the great critic Jan Kreustadt pushed his way forward to inspect the canvas. He shouted: "This is a *blank canvas* you idiots!" In an apoplectic rage he hurled his wine glass at the work, leaving four ounces of 1969 Château Mouton Rothschild dripping over the canvas.

Kinski excitedly ran up to his defaced work and yelled: "Nixon's an alcoholic! It's Perfect!" After a bidding war, the work sold that night for $15,000, considerably more than the original list price of $2,500.

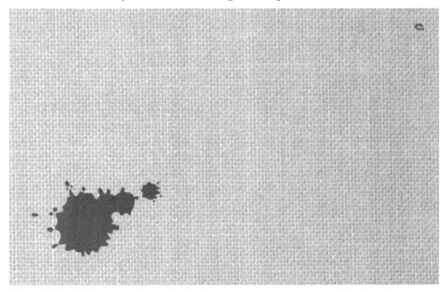

Nixon's Mind (1974), Dan Loathitz Collection, the Art Institute of Weehawken.

"Genuine Forgeries"

The success of his Oblique series, and the notoriety of *Nixon's Mind*, made Kinski the New York art world's sensation of 1974. It rekindled interest in Kinski's earlier work. Auction houses were selling works even from his forgotten period of the 1940s, 50s, and 60s for outrageous prices.

This set the stage for Kinski's role in the "Genuine Forgeries" scandal of early 1975. Art historians are still debating the extent of Kinski's role in the scandal.

Kinski had sold many of his early works during his lean decades. Now after the *Nixon's Mind* incident, he discovered that he owned very few of his own paintings. Although he could sell even despised works, such as *Edsel in Oils* (1952), for good money, he had adopted a lavish lifestyle and was soon out of funds. He had also sunk most of his money into ill-fated investments like General Motors, whose stock was then plummeting in the wake of the OPEC oil embargo.

It was in this context that Kinski became vulnerable to the scheme of a scrofulous character named Phil Betcher, a fledgling painter, who insinuated himself into Kinski's newly formed entourage. Betcher devised a scheme whereby Kinski would sign his name to Betcher's works, claim he had executed the works years before, and then sell them to the unwitting auction houses.

Unfortunately, this scheme was not uncovered until after Kinski's death in November, 1975. Until that time, Betcher painted furiously, sometimes producing as many as three works per day for Kinski's signature: bleary emulsion painting, oils, watercolors, and even sketches (though Kinski himself was more of a concept artist and not known to have sketched anything). Kinski himself churned out some fast, second-rate work during this time. He often gave them anti-Nixon titles (*Adolph Nixon*, *Dick Head*, *What's a Dick For?*), even when no human forms were discernible within the work. These were purchased eagerly by the auction houses, and later by individual collectors.

We now have some 5,000 paintings nominally painted by Kinski, but since his signature is on all of them, it is nearly impossible to distinguish the real Kinski's from the "genuine forgeries" he signed for Betcher. Some scholars claim the ability to tell Kinski's work from Betcher's, but hopelessly confusing matters is the fact that the respected critic Irving Hanneman actually witnessed Kinski executing several Betcher-like paintings. Hanneman believed that Betcher influenced Kinski's late style! For many, Betcher, who spent years studying at the Sorbonne, was actually a far more technically proficient artist than Kinski, who was self-taught, and a poor draftsman.

Final Days: Hair Piece

Still, throughout 1974-75, Kinski was seen as an elder statesman within the American art scene. He was diagnosed with terminal cancer in April, 1975. In his magisterial June, 1975 *Playboy* interview he summarized his place in American art:

> I know what Americans like. Americans like attacks on Richard Nixon, floating clocks [a reference to Dali's *Persistence of Memory*, a favorite Kinski/Betcher theme] and the slaughter of innocent children on television. Except for pockets of New York City, America is a very anti-artistic society. By attacking the stale conventions of twentieth century art, I have attempted to give the people what they want.

Kinski remained an artist to the end, and visitors to the Warner Gallery were privileged to see his final work of art, *Hair Piece,* an actual strand of white hair that he yanked out of his head while on his deathbed, and scotch-taped to the wall above the nightstand. Reputedly, he uttered: "Though my corpse will be too wasted to leave to science, I shall leave my body to art!" He stretched to affix the strand of hair to the wall, and then he died.

Kinski's Legacy

Assessing Kinski's legacy remains problematic. One can now find his works in museums throughout the world, and yet a cloud of uncertainty hangs over his *oeuvre*. Without running chemical dating tests on the 5,000 or so suspect canvasses it is impossible to determine which works are truly Kinski's. Museum curators and private collectors are understandably chary of such tests, which could only depreciate the paper value of their collections by millions of dollars. And so, while it is difficult to sell Kinski's works, the high asking price for the more famous pieces still drives up the value of probable Betcher forgeries signed by Kinski.

Yet his place in twentieth century American art is assured. Although his forgotten thirty-year "middle period" is of little value, works from his early and late periods remain charming and memorable salvos against the pretentiousness of representational art, and even against supposedly revolutionary movements such as Cubism.

"Karl Kinski: Arbitrary Expressionist" will move to Chicago, and then to Seattle, before the pieces are returned to their permanent collections.

Felix Spielenhammer: "The Heavy Mahler"

The great German composer and musicologist Felix Spielenhammer left an indelible mark on musical history. His development as a composer and theorist mirrors developments in twentieth century music as a whole. His death was mourned by true music lovers everywhere.

Although he began composing at the age of five, Spielenhammer's creative output was small considering his nearly 100 years of life. Aside from his masterpiece, the incomparable "Cacophonous Symphony" (*Opus No. 4 in F*

Minor), he produced only two piano concertos, one violin concerto, one movie soundtrack, one completely disastrous opera, two musical comedies (one never produced), a TV theme song, and a mound of unfinished scraps of music, some of which he later admitted should never have been performed publicly. But aside from his musical output, Spielenhammer published several volumes on the theory of music that influenced many 20th Century composers.

Spielenhammer: Early Life

In a long life replete with the most absurd ironies, it comes as no surprise that Spielenhammer, like many artists, grew up in the midst of an unusual family life. Felix, born on April 1, 1897 in Essen, Germany, was the only son of "Mad" Rudolf Spielenhammer and his wife, Brigitte. Spielenhammer's sister, Cosima, was born in 1900. The Spielenhammers lived in terrible poverty throughout young Felix's childhood, supported only by Brigitte's job in a munitions factory. "Mad" Rudolf had been stone-deaf since the age of ten, but tried reluctantly to earn a living through a series of odd jobs: coachmen, bartender, butler, numbers runner, and piano-tuner.

The Spielenhammers lived in a noisy one-room flat next to the railroad tracks in the town of Essen. The family was outcast, chiefly because of Mad Rudolf's scandalous reputation, which he earned during violent drinking bouts that often landed him in the local jail. Mad Rudolf was known to visit prostitutes, assault the town constable, and disrupt masses with loud and outrageous claims about Pope Leo XIII's excessive appetite for cold cuts. He also shrieked like an animal in the town square at all hours. He had married Brigitte, the cherished daughter of a wealthy merchant family, on the strength of 100,000 *Reichsmarks* he had won at the roulette wheel in Baden-Baden. Her family forced her on young Rudolf, because—though beautiful—she was still unwed at the age of 25.

But with the gambling winnings quickly spent on Rudolf's vices, and with two young children to support, Brigitte was forced to take a job as a drill-press operator at the local Krupp Munitions plant—an unusual occupation for a married woman in Wilhelmine Germany. Fearful of leaving her young children with Mad Rudolf, Brigitte brought her young children with her to the munitions plant, where they were treated to the harsh sounds of riveting and pounding machines for ten hours a day, six days a week. Musicologists believe that this experience was to have a lasting impression on young Felix, whose works were later to feature clanging disharmonies, deafening discordance, and an excessive use of violent cymbal smashing, among other obnoxiously loud noises.

But the infant Felix was also exposed to more melodious sounds. Brigitte herself was a competent pianist, and spent her Sunday afternoons teaching the young boy how to play on the family piano. Although he was prone to pounding the instrument harshly, seemingly in imitation of the sounds he heard during the week, young Felix soon mastered a few basic keys, and by the age of four could play fairly reputable renditions of popular German folk songs.

In the midst of this terrible squalor, young Felix became the only hope of their desperate lives. At age six he composed his first popular melody, entitled *Armlicher Mann, Sehr Sehr Armlicher Mann* ("Poor Man, Really Really Poor Man"), which, when copyrighted and published, brought the desperate family some extra income. However, Mad Rudolf squandered most of Felix's royalties at the roulette wheel.

Young Felix soon began attending the local school where his peers subjected him to violent taunting about his ugliness. He had inherited his father's snub nose and beady eyes, and even at the age of five seemed to possess a receding hairline. His atrocious wardrobe didn't help matters. Felix was soon in the throes of despair, and even refused to play the instrument he already had come to love. Brigitte was powerless to get the boy to return to the piano, her efforts only earning her various projectile food offerings, as young Felix hurled plates of potatoes or *Spätzle* at her in disgust. Brigitte's attempts to teach young Cosima the piano were totally fruitless, as the young girl, though possessed of perfect hearing, pretended to mimic her father's deafness out of some misguided sense of pro-fatherly love.

Despite a gnawing sense of social inferiority, Felix eventually returned to the piano, spending countless hours on the instrument and achieving a technical competency—albeit far from virtuosity—that far outstripped his mother's. Felix's teachers found him idiotic and eccentric and doubted he would ever amount to much. One teacher even wrote he would make "excellent canon-fodder" should war break out between Germany and France. Cosima proved unmanageable early on, trying to incite even her kindergarten class to sing "Deutschland über Alles."

By the eve of the First World War Spielenhammer's abilities had attracted notice from the neighboring nobility. Count Max von Lothringen Rheingold became his patron. Felix accompanied Count Rheingold to St. Petersburg in the spring of 1913, and music legend has it that young Spielenhammer was the first of many spectators to throw fruit at the musicians during the first public performance of Igor Stravinsky's *The Rites of Spring*—declared a masterpiece only twenty years later. But Felix fell in love with the musical culture of St. Petersburg. At the age of sixteen he spent a night in prison for running wildly down the streets of the capital yelling: "Tchaikovsky is God!"

When war broke out in the summer of 1914, Spielenhammer, though only seventeen, managed to enlist in the Prussian army. He was soon stationed on the Western front. His front line division was subject to nearly constant bombardment by a powerful battery of British artillery, and casualties ran high. Spielenhammer himself, however, was to emerge from the war without a scratch, his fellow soldiers reporting that he would scribble feverishly on music paper throughout the bombardments, as if at the peak of inspiration.

Spielenhammer returned to Essen after the Armistice of 1918 to find his family in worse circumstances than ever. Mad Rudolf's mocking efforts to master the violin had only earned him fierce beatings from enraged neighbors, and his profligate spending had grown uncontrollable. By now Rudolf was banned from all music stores within a 50 kilometer radius, and most other shops as well. The family's debts were by now astronomical and could never be repaid, and the piano and most of the furniture had long been carried off by embittered creditors. Brigitte had grown weaker from long hours at the Krupp plant, and from her desperate attempts to keep the family together. Cosima had dropped out of school, and was destined to marry the village idiot, an unkempt, mysterious creature known only as "Fritz."

Mad Rudolf wept uncontrollably on seeing his son return from the war. When Brigitte explained that his father had been counting on receiving Felix's military pension after the boy's expected death in battle, Spielenhammer became completely disillusioned with his family. He received a stipend from the aging Count Rheingold to study music in Vienna, and after promising to send his mother some money, he was soon on a train for the music capital of the world.

Early Career

Armed with Count Rheingold's stipend, young Spielenhammer soon began to slip into the debauchery of his father, spending much of his funds on the high-class prostitutes that lined Vienna's Ringstrasse. His auditions at the finer conservatories proved disastrous. The young pianist was obviously very nervous, and one judge simply wrote "Ach, die Pein! die Pein!" ("Oh, the agony!") on Spielenhammer's evaluation form. Meanwhile, Spielenhammer supported himself as a piano tutor.

His first break came when he decided to attend a public lecture given by the innovator of atonal composition, the great Arnold Schoenberg. Schoenberg's revolutionary "atonal" theory of music held that the traditional eight-tone octave structure should be scrapped in favor of a revolutionary, if less melodic, twelve-tone structure. Schoenberg and the atonalists that followed were to enjoy great appreciation among music lovers during the course of the twentieth century.

But Spielenhammer, a fiery twenty-one year old by 1918, was soon viewed as a radical even by Schoenberg and his disciples. Spielenhammer, after ingratiating himself into Schoenberg's circle, quickly argued that music should not be grounded on any kind of traditional scale whatsoever, but should aim to reflect the sounds that the modern working man was likely to hear in his daily life. To illustrate his point Spielenhammer quickly composed his now infamous *Opus No. 4 in No Key*, which, through its use of clanging disharmonies, earsplitting discords—as well as railroad, industrial and even animal sounds—was to set the world of music on its head.

Before the first public performance of *Opus No. 4*, Spielenhammer published a musical treatise entitled *Der Klang des Klanges* (*The Sound of Sound*) which attempted to prepare musical audiences for the thunderbolt he was about to unleash on the world of music. First published in the Vienna *Zeitung*, Spielenhammer's seminal article argued that:

> *Modern* music should represent the anarchy of modern life; it must be structure-less, spontaneous, and unpredictable. No longer is man in nature. He no longer hears singing birds. Operatic *arias* and chamber music are purely for sissies. What we deem to be beautiful in music is, as in all art, simply a product of our breeding. If heard often enough, even fingernails scratching a chalkboard—again and again and again—will begin to sound pleasant to us, even comforting in a way. (*The Sound of Sound*, 24)

Although Schoenberg and the more respected composers of Vienna soon denounced Spielenhammer as "an obvious fraud," news of a revolutionary breakthrough in music had brought the anticipation for the opening of *Opus No. 4 in No Key* to a fever pitch.

Performing the *Opus* placed completely unprecedented demands on the orchestra, as the more traditional string and wind instruments were joined by a vast and motley assortment of other objects capable of sound. To stage his production, Spielenhammer was forced to write a desperate letter to Count Rheingold—now, by all accounts, completely senile—for financial backing. But with the necessary funds soon in hand, Spielenhammer was able to procure all the things he needed to stage his masterpiece. He was to stage it outdoors at noontime, on October 30, 1919, near the large fountain of the Ringstrasse in Vienna's center. Admittance was free to the public.

Besides the traditional orchestra, Spielenhammer's requirements for performing his *Opus* included:

> 10 large gongs, 4 kettle drums with industrial-strength skins, a sex-starved cow, several recently soiled babies, 3 old Mercedes with inoperable starters, a Howitzer cannon, several rounds of explosives, a cat, a bathtub, a harmonica, a hairy man needing a bandage removed, five divorcees with vindictive streaks who have recently quit smoking, an incompetent bugle player, and an unwashed duck.

October 30th proved to be a sunny day, ideal for a noontime concert. Vendors sold beer and sausages from sidewalk stands.

From the first violent bangs on the gongs by some unruly delinquents—hand-picked by Spielenhammer himself—audiences knew they were in for something special. The violin section began playing something sounding suspiciously like *The 1812 Overture* while the wind section simultaneously played the opening theme from Beethoven's *Fifth Symphony*. Spielenhammer, perched on a high, specially constructed platform, made wild gestures with his unusually large baton, gesturing for everyone to play louder, and when unsatisfied, approached the musicians and began randomly exchanging their music with others while the performance continued, inducing sheer chaos in the string section. Simultaneously he made violent gestures to his numerous "sound crew," who attempted to start the Mercedes, speak rationally to the vindictive divorcees, change the babies, wash the cat, help the man remove his bandage, fire the cannon, ignite the dynamite, and do unspeakable things with the harmonica and the duck.

The entire performance lasted a scant nine minutes, most of the professional musicians deserting about halfway through, leaving the "sound crew" to continue the performance unsupported by the orchestra. Only now was it understood why Spielenhammer had strictly forbade any rehearsals. As the musicians fled *en masse*, Spielenhammer was heard to shout "Fine! It's better without you!" and shake his fist angrily at them, before resuming his conducting with even more maniacal energy.

The large noontime audience was at first curious, then perplexed, and eventually enraged by the thought they had been swindled. Some of the Viennese began to charge Spielenhammer's platform, but his loyal delinquents were able to whisk the conductor away by miraculously starting up one of the old Mercedes and driving him away from the angry mob at top speed.

Spielenhammer had quickly become the first *persona non grata* in the newly formed state of Austria. Franz Schuler, the conductor of Vienna's prestigious *Staatsoper* (State Opera), publicly petitioned the mayor to have him banned from Vienna for life.

Fleeing to the newly formed Weimar Republic of Germany, Spielenhammer justified himself and his music in a long newspaper article entitled "On the Idiocy of the Viennese." Here he pilloried Vienna as being "a city *beyond* decadence," and lambasted their "resistance to innovation" in music.

But Spielenhammer found himself much more at home in Weimar Germany—perhaps the most decadent flowering of German culture of all time. Although his music publisher was willing to publish the score of *Opus No. 4*, critics were perplexed by the relative lack of musical notation. Heinrich Fischer warned readers that:

> We find nothing in Spielenhammer's *Opus* that can be called serious music. Instead we only find a long list of 'instruments' and instructions: 'bang drum fiercely,' 'beat cow,' 'fire cannon,' 'play Beethoven atrociously.' All in all it doesn't add up to much. It is obviously intended to be something 'beyond music,' a critique of all that is 'too orderly and rigid' in traditional harmonic structures.

> After a bad day at the office, Schoenberg is quite tolerable, even cathartic; but Spielenhammer simply goes too far.

Although embittered by the poor public reception of his new "meta-music," Spielenhammer, vowing to make a living as a composer at all costs, quickly returned to more traditional forms, and began writing for the then growing musical theater circuit in Berlin. His first musical comedy, a merry romp entitled *Hansel and Gretel Underground*, was a continuation of the popular German fairy tale. The young children, after following a misleading trail of breadcrumbs, are trapped by a sinister wolf/entrepreneur named "Yeastless Ludwig," and forced to work long hours in his *Wunderbrot* bread factory.

Despite its serious themes and scathing social commentary, *Hansel* featured such memorable popular songs as the rollicking "We Eat Too Much," and the naughty "Why, Tell Me Why, Is Incest So Wrong?" Even Yeastless Ludwig is given to song, and his touching solos "Gretel, my Gretel," and the gut-wrenching "Who Put the 'Bad' in the 'Big Bad Wolf?'" offer tragic interludes in an otherwise farcical musical comedy. Although touching on such forbidden themes as bestiality and incest, the bulk of *Hansel and Gretel Underground* is comprised of spritely, comedic numbers, as Spielenhammer successfully kept the play from degenerating into the "ponderous critique of industrialism" that one critic saw in the work.

Flushed with the minor success of *Hansel*, Spielenhammer felt professionally secure enough to marry his first wife, Lotte Karlsbad, a former prostitute turned singer-actress. Lotte's first professional acting job was the role of Yeastless Ludwig's pet iguana in *Hansel*. Some doubted the wisdom of the marriage. Felix's friend, Franz Kruger, described Lotte as "literally a slut," and predicted marital disaster should Spielenhammer's career ever suffer the slightest downturn.

Although *Hansel* had seemingly given him years of financial security, the winter of 1922-23 saw the worst outbreak of hyper-inflation in German history. The savings of most middle class families were completely wiped out. A loaf of bread now cost a wheelbarrow full of *Reichsmarks*. Workers had to be given large pay raises of increasingly worthless money—almost daily—to keep up with spiraling costs.

But as a composer, Spielenhammer had no steady wages to rely on. *Hansel* was soon canceled, and many theaters shut down completely. The newlyweds were now desperate, and Lotte threatened to resume her former profession if Felix did not take swift action.

His response to this threat was the creation of the never-produced musical comedy *Fame and Famine*, which featured such distasteful songs as "Brother, Can You Spare 1.8 Million *Reichsmarks*?" and the scandalous "Maggie the Spoon"—which to his dying day Spielenhammer fiercely avowed had been stolen by the young Kurt Weill, and later transformed into the wildly successful "Mack the Knife."

Middle Years

With his royalties from *Really, Really Poor Man* and *Hansel* now being paid to him in almost worthless German currency, Spielenhammer fled to the United States in the spring of 1924, accompanied by Lotte. His former "association" with the great Schoenberg gave him access to the elite music circles of the United States, which discounted Schoenberg's daily, denunciatory trans-Atlantic telegrams about Spielenhammer as mere "artistic quarreling." He was embraced as yet another German musical genius.

But exactly at this time we see the beginnings of a strange lull in Spielenhammer's musical output. Although he was offered handsome sums to produce a musical comedy, or indeed any complete musical piece for New York audiences, he simply could not write music any more—"not one note" as he was to complain in his journals. Perhaps he could not adapt to American culture. Perhaps he was jarred when Lotte inexplicably slapped him in the face one night and left him forever—musicologists still debate the issue.

A grief-struck Spielenhammer, whose musical output was scant during his eight years in America, took a professorship in music at the City College of New York. Here he began work on a definitive, multi-volume theory of music, entitled *A Theory of Music*, which is now considered a milestone in musicology.

Spielenhammer argued that a piece of music should be first understood and listened to as a story:

> It has long been understood that the rhythm and pitch of music determines its mood: happy, playful, ponderous, angry, or triumphant. But rarely has it been understood that music can and should be used to convey the entire story of a man's life. The progressive rhythms of a piece—often *largo* then *andante* then *allegro* then *vivace* then *moderato* then silence—signify the stages of man's existence—the womb, infancy, childhood, maturity, middle-age, and our final decay. (*A Theory of Music*, 214)

A Theory of Music contains more famous quotations: "the greater the grief it induces in us, the greater the piece of music"; "music should make us hate the composer—for his genius"; "I hate most other composers and musicians. I really do"; "great music should cause great sorrow."

Although it was little read and poorly received on its publication in 1927, *A Theory of Music* influenced later generations of composers. Although many bemoaned the rambling, four hundred pages Spielenhammer devoted to his personal problems, his more germane discussions of music were "a breath of fresh air" for the young Shostakovich, among many others.

Despite ominous warnings from his German correspondents and friends, Spielenhammer decided to return to Germany in January, 1933—just in time for the Nazi Dictatorship. He arrived in Essen on January 30, 1933, the very day that the *Reichstag* was burned down in Berlin, precipitating the end of democratic rule. Many German musicians and artists were fleeing Germany just as Spielenhammer returned.

He discovered his parents in better circumstances than before. Even some of the old debts had been repaid. Both Felix and Cosima had been sending them checks. Cosima now earned a solid living as a ghost writer for the Ministry of Propaganda. Fritz, predictably, was unemployed.

Faced with the prospect of seeing Mad Rudolf all day, Brigitte had been reluctant to quit her job at Krupp, but the Gestapo's tactics of discouraging women in the workforce eventually persuaded her. Rudolf, although physically healthy, had taken to lying in bed until mid-afternoon, having Brigitte serve him coffee and read him the newspaper.

Meanwhile, Spielenhammer was being courted by the Ministry of Propaganda to produce pro-Nazi music for public consumption. Spielenhammer, who lived in America during Hitler's rise to power and so was totally ignorant of his racist program, was at first impressed by the Nazis: that they had restored the shattered pride of the Fatherland and had created plenty of jobs. Later, as their violent anti-Semitism became more obvious, Spielenhammer refused to write the propagandistic music they demanded.

Spielenhammer's disillusionment with the Nazis prompted his emigration to Britain, where he was to spend the Second World War. Cosima, still at Propaganda, declared her brother officially insane, but still appropriated some of his German copyrighted music for parades and marches. She published new arrangements of his music, enclosing preposterous Nazi-inspired interpretations. Cosima described Yeastless Ludwig from *Hansel* as a symbol of wolf-like Western-style capitalism and imperialism. Hansel and Gretel themselves were apparently symbols of the comparatively innocent and oppressed countries of Germany and Italy.

Spielenhammer was outraged at this use of works, but from 1939 on, with war raging in Europe, he was powerless to intervene. Although now seen as somewhat suspect in the West, Spielenhammer was to produce some of his best music during the war. His *Piano Concerto No. 1* displayed his characteristic originality in orchestration, featuring an average of one symbol smash per measure, and unexpected stretches of complete silence that musicologists believe reveal a more contemplative and meditative Spielenhammer; others say he was simply short of ideas, and had to fill time. Regardless, Spielenhammer's use of silence was to influence many twentieth-century composers, most notably the American John Cage, whose *Four Minutes and Thirty-Three Seconds* featured total silence for its duration, baffling many an audience, but providing musicologists and aestheticians with infinite fodder for speculation.

The war years were to be the most prolific years of Spielenhammer's career. He attempted to illustrate the principles he had set out in *A Theory of*

Music, producing a slew of "biographical musicals" about Beethoven, Napoleon, Byron, Goethe, and Bertrand Russell (though *Why I Am Not a Christian: The Musical* was never produced).

After the war, in 1947, Spielenhammer staged his only opera, *Day Becomes Night*, which dealt with his childhood with astonishing frankness. The opera's characters—"Mad" Rolf, Gretchen, Felix, Cosima and Fritz, were obviously thinly veiled characterizations of Spielenhammer's family. By now the real Cosima and Fritz had fled to Argentina, where one day they would make a fortune by staging Spielenhammer's long-forgotten *Fame and Famine*, which appealed to Argentine audiences during their years of hyper-inflation in the 1960s and 70s. But *Day Becomes Night* centered on the character of "Mad" Rolf, especially his drinking and carousing. Rolf, however, is seen as a victim, and is given to eloquent soliloquies on life's meaning, which for him becomes the systematic avoidance of all work and effort. Predictably, Cosima emerges as the villain, as seen in her efforts to steal Gretchen's wages for Fritz' outlandish inventions—such as a car that runs on brainwaves.

But Spielenhammer himself was not to maintain his creative output. By the early 1950s we find him copyrighting single stanzas of music—hundreds of them—which he was simply incapable of merging into any creative whole. He was appointed Professor of Music at Weimar, but was only able to perform his duties for a few years. But he began teaching from his *Theory of Music*, and eventually was to convince other professors to make his book a standard work.

By 1960, Spielenhammer was retired, and became a recluse, rarely emerging from his villa near Hanover. Visitors would find the aging genius in an appalling state, his villa a disturbing scene of filth and clutter. Three years of mail was strewn about, mostly unopened. Apparently the composer was subsisting only on bread and goat's milk, and not enough of either, for he was emaciated and apparently dying.

But in the increasingly radical 1960s, musicians were taking a closer look at Spielenhammer's life's work, and began to hail him as a suppressed, revolutionary musical genius. His works sold by the thousands and became standard fare for university courses. Theaters in Hamburg, West Berlin, Weimar, Bonn, and Heidelberg performed *Hansel and Gretel Underground*, and even the forgotten *Opus No. 4 in No Key* was being hailed on both sides of the iron curtain as masterpiece of modern realism. Spielenhammer was soon a truly wealthy man for the first time, and after fortifying himself with an eccentric diet and exercise regimen, emerged for his first public appearance in over ten years.

He settled in West Berlin, where he quickly became a public nuisance for the authorities, staging absurd anti-nuclear protests: short-lived (afternoon) hunger strikes, poorly attended protests and brief marches—all featuring shocking accusations about the covert activities of the U.S. government. He failed in his many efforts to get himself arrested.

Final Years

Spielenhammer's appetite for political activism did not outlast the 1960s. A new "revisionary" movement in musicology deemed Spielenhammer "an unadulterated fraud," and even his well-established tome, *A Theory of Music*, was out of print by 1972.

Spielenhammer, now in his seventies, vowed to never perform publicly again, nor to publish any new pieces—a somewhat idle threat considering he hadn't published a stanza since 1961. But with his solidified wealth Spielenhammer, in his last public statement, vowed he would now "enjoy life." A year later we find him married, this time to Danya Alexandrovna, a ravishing young music student, ostensibly smitten by Spielenhammer's former genius.

Documentation on the last ten years of Spielenhammer's life is strangely unavailable. Scholars have been forced to rely on the word of Danya, who has described him as "a gentle flower in need of almost constant care and attention." Despite the demands of caring for her husband, Danya has remained very much in the public eye, often appearing in the celebrity pages of *Der Spiegel*, dressed to the nines, and eating in Hamburg's finest restaurants with handsome young men—"admirers of my husband" in Danya's own words.

Spielenhammer's Legacy

Assessing Spielenhammer's place in musical history remains a problematic task. Although he enjoyed periods of near world fame, from another perspective his was a transient inspiration, a small flame in the dark torpor of musical stagnation. He lacks the synthetic brilliance of the world's greatest composers. He was more of a bad boy of music, someone willing to test the boundaries of what "music" really is, perhaps just to show us how much we enjoy the real thing.

Alexandria Czechtealeaves: True Psychic

Alexandria Czechtealeaves, a humble orange rind collector from Pensacola, Florida, muttered some of the most astonishing predictions in modern psychic history.

Alexandria's recent death prompted hysterical weeping from her millions of followers. Some even made the pilgrimage to Pensacola—in denial about her death—and hoping to catch a glimpse of the hunched old woman as she foraged through dumpsters, in search of prophetic orange rinds.

Alexandria's utterances have been faithfully transcribed by a young leper called Misha, who had previously distinguished himself as Assistant Secretary of Housing and Urban Development. Misha has just published Alexandria's predictions as *The Prophecies of Alexandria: The Role of Citrus Fruits in Determining Global Mega-Trends*. From prolonged meditation upon the bumps in navel oranges, Alexandria shocked the world with her predictions.

Her first recorded prediction was published in the *Tampa Daily News* in September, 1983. As she and Misha were being arrested for trying to suffocate each other with cheesecloth, Alexandria mumbled something in an unknown tongue which Misha translated as: "Toshiro will soon die." Amazingly, Toshiro Mifune of Tokyo, the world's oldest living person at 117 years of age, died later that day when his frail frame slid into his toilet, and was flushed into oblivion by his vindictive cat, Louis. The Tampa papers published her prediction, and a public outcry led to her and Misha's early release.

At the televised press conference that followed, Alexandria garbled more prophecies in her strange, grating speech that one linguistics professor in attendance declared was Classical Sanskrit, and another said was caused by her strange practice of a holding a Slinky between her gums as a low-cost denture-substitute. Luckily, Misha was on hand to translate her latest prophecies:

> Population growth will continue. By the year 2020 there will probably be "many more" human beings.
>
> Many new brands of condiments will continue to be marketed each year, especially salad dressings.
>
> America will never pay off its national debt.
>
> Chevy Chase will never win an Academy Award for Best Actor.
>
> There will never be a nuclear holocaust during our lifetimes.

"Alex," as she was affectionately called by her new disciples, soon appeared on many television shows, along with Misha who served as her translator. Audiences were delighted by her predictions that Oprah Winfrey would not make the U.S. Olympic swim team, and that Phil Donahue would be declared a deity in an unnamed Latin American country.

But it was her appearance on "Geraldo" that made national headlines. She had been choking on her Slinky dentures, when Misha performed the Heimlich maneuver on her, causing her to turn and catapult the steel coil into the startled face of Geraldo, who wet himself. Geraldo, in a froth, smashed the Slinky to bits, inciting the toothless "Alex" to bite his moustache off with her gums, while Misha stood on stage, pelting him with salamanders. Misha then told the audience that this incident was a sign from God that U.S. steel production was declining, and that America was converting itself to a service-oriented economy. The next day, this prediction was confirmed in the *Wall Street Journal*.

Despite her repute, Alex was forced to write out fortune cookies for a living. But her life of destitution ended in December 1987, when she and Misha were summoned to the White House by President Ronald Reagan. Reagan had recently locked all his chief economists and his astrologers together in a meat locker, and was shopping around for new advisors.

Misha told Reagan Alex's prediction that Reagan would be elected to a second term, a prediction that seemed to delight the President. When Nancy Reagan pointed out that her husband was already serving his second term, Misha lashed out at her as "an unbeliever" and predicted that Nancy would one day be swallowed whole by her own goldfish; the frightened President immediately increased her Secret Service detail.

Misha also told the President that he should refuse ABC's offer for him to appear on the TV quiz show "Jeopardy" and compete against a dolphin, a head of cabbage, and a wax sculpture; his chances of victory, said Misha, were "not good." Reagan accepted this prudent advice. He thanked Misha and Alex, and as a token of his gratitude he gave her a set of wooden teeth. Misha was offered the state of Rhode Island but declined.

The Bush Administration also sought Alex's advice. However, she was fired after Misha asserted that Barbara Bush was really President Bush's grandmother and that as a child the future President had appeared on TV's *The Mickey Mouse Club* as one of the "Mouseketeers." These claims were demonstrably untrue. Unemployed, the psychic team returned to Pensacola.

A tent-city of Alex's admirers had sprung up in Pensacola. They proclaimed her God and bought her a 1979 Ford Pinto. Soon, before a hushed gathering at a Pensacola delicatessen, Misha gave the somber news that Alex had predicted her own death after looking into a glass of Tang instant breakfast drink. She had named Misha as her successor and left him all her earthly belongings. The next day, Misha reported that Alex and the Pinto were missing, and in a year she was pronounced dead. But her body was never found, giving rise to rumors that she was still alive, gobbling Fig Newtons and serving as a staffer for the World Health Organization.

Misha turned down several Cabinet level positions in order to form a political lobby, fighting for full health insurance for lepers. He can still be seen on TV in the center square on "Hollywood Squares," and sometimes peddling his psychic hotline.

Misha's publication of her collected prophecies has renewed interest in this remarkable woman, known to so many as just plain "Alex."

Hans Donkerzijde's Amsterdam City Gate

One of the great what-ifs of Amsterdam "Golden Age" architecture was Hans Donkerzijde's audacious design for a portal on the east side of the city. Donkerzijde (1613-1678) intended his portal to be both the acme of all previous golden-age Dutch architecture as well as a radical break with known styles. Donkerzijde designed his portal *(poort)* as a monument to his own genius. His manic drive to build the greatest portal in Amsterdam sprang from his lifelong drive for recognition.

Early Life

He began his apprenticeship as a bricklayer at the age of 14, worked long hours of labor, and vowed to rise in society—despite his obvious social inadequacies. Descriptions of him by contemporaries leave an impression of a man whose emotional range ran the spectrum from fear to arrogance. "I find his gaze extremely unsettling. His beady eyes dart around my face, as if scanning me for weak points," wrote Daan Goudsmit, his long-time assistant.

It's unclear exactly what turned around Donkerzijde's fortunes, but sometime between 1635 and 1637, Donkerzijde found the time and resources to travel to Rome. Upon his return he set up his own office, and began receiving commissions.

Scholars have unearthed documents establishing that Donkerzijde had joined a secret society around 1635, which might explain his sudden ascent in the world. Donkerzijde became a member of the *Geheim Donker Genootschap* (GDG) ("secret dark brotherhood"), whose history and goals remain unclear to historians. This sparked wild speculation and conspiracy theorizing among historians.[13]

The GDG reputedly met in an anonymous room in a warehouse near the Driehoek, the corner of the Brouwersgracht (Brewer's Canal) and Lijnbaansgracht. This intersection formed the apex of a large triangle on the city grid in the *Jordaan* section of Amsterdam. The grid formed a series of progressively larger triangles, a shape that fascinated Donkerzijde throughout his life.

Donkerzijde's Amsterdam Town Hall

In 1647 he submitted a design for the new Amsterdam town hall. Donkerzijde's design—crudely derivative of the Pantheon in Rome—used alternating bell and step gables to cradle the massive sphere. His design made him a laughingstock, and mentioning "Donkerzijde's folly" was good for a laugh in architectural circles even years later.

Twentieth century Dutch art historian Jaap van den Brink argues that the blueprint of "the so-called Dutch Pantheon" was in fact a primitive attempt at Dadaism:

---

[13] Historians including Francois Boulanger have seen the Geheim Donker Genootschap (GDG) as a kind of "Freemasonry light," lacking their illustrious history and depth, and revering only a mere triangle (as opposed to the Freemasons' three-dimensional pyramid). Others have rejected this explanation and see the GDG as a coterie of Catholic businessmen, meeting secretly out of sheer paranoia. Herman van Utrecht conceives something far more sinister, based on anecdotal evidence that William III himself was an ultra-secret member of the GDG (level 13 out of 13). Utrecht argues that they were really a conspiracy of Protestant international bankers, *hiding behind* a Catholic secret society. According to this theory, Donkerzijde was only a dupe, and had no knowledge of the GDG's long-term plot to control the world's money supply, by establishing the first stock exchange in Amsterdam and later the Bank of England in London (established by the Dutchman, William III, as King of England, in 1694).

[his] audacity to include even the oculus [the all-weather hole in the roof] in the rain-soaked United Provinces was clearly not the work of a man who intended to secure a contract. Donkerzijde could not have been serious; he was satirizing the nepotism of the city's elites, knowing the utter futility of his winning the bid (*Encyclopedia of Minor Dutch Architects*, 13).

His grand interior called for a massive fresco inspired by Michelangelo's *The Last Judgment*. He creates a conceit of civic pride by showing Amsterdam (as seen in Cornelis Anthonisz's already-dated 1544 "bird's-eye" woodcut of the city) floating up to heaven, higher even than the great cities of antiquity: Jerusalem, Babylon, Athens, and Rome. God Himself can be seen smiling upon Amsterdam's fortunes and pointing at the city with special favor. (Clearly the Lord is not bothered by the city's trade in women, tobacco and beer.) The design also describes a marble inlay floor depicting a giant map of Europe with Amsterdam as its center—right under the oculus.

When van Campen's own marble hemisphere floors were unveiled in the *Burgerzaal* years later, Donkerzijde cried foul, and remained bitter for the rest of his days, convinced that his ideas had been stolen.

Donkerzijde's Muiderpoort

For the next twenty years, Donkerzijde struggled along, building mainly footbridges in outlying areas. By 1671, aged 58, Donkerzijde still had not created any architectural legacy of note. That year, he was convinced by a deceptive land speculator, Joost van Os, that the east side of Amsterdam would soon experience a great financial boom, rivaling even the tulip mania of 1621, which Donkerzijde remembered from his boyhood.

In expectation, Donkerzijde invested his life's savings in some swampy land near the *Plantage* side of town. He envisioned the *Muiderpoort* as the gateway to the east, and to the great city's future. Although relatively little traffic came through the Muiderpoort in those days, Donkerzijde convinced the city fathers that a small duty on loads entering through the gate could win back building costs—which he promised to hold under tight control.

Donkerzijde's audacious design for the Muiderpoort called for three grand *triangular* archways (Donkerzijde never mastered his triangle fixation) made largely in brick. The great gables would be surrounded by seven meter tall sculptures of the great heroes of the young Dutch Republic's history: William the Silent, de Ruijter, Vondel, and others. (For political reasons, he agreed to replace his proposed statue of Oldenbarnevelt with Maurits.) The outer walls were to feature immense gryphon, much like those that were later to grace the gates to the City of London.

There were, however, a few irksome problems to be solved before construction could begin. First, there already *was* a functional city gate in place on Donkerzijde's chosen site, completed only in 1663, a mere eight years prior. True, it had been rather hastily constructed after the frenzied push to expand the canal belt (*grachtengordel*), but no one was complaining about it. Amsterdammers had pride enough in their rich architectural splendor: the new town hall, the great churches and canal houses. So yet another new city gate, near the least settled part of town, had not even been considered.

In order to maintain the operation of the current Muiderpoort, Donkerzijde planned to construct his own massive portal *over* it, and then knock down the old one when he was finished building. Construction began in 1671 with the strengthening of the foundation via the time-honored method of driving wooden piles into the soft clay and peat.

Donkerzijde's longtime draftsman, Daan Goudsmit calculated that not nearly enough piles had been driven to safely support the structure long term. He found the design so outrageous that he resigned in protest, writing with barely concealed contempt that:

> ...your design, sir, violates core principles both of architecture and of natural philosophy. Can this watery foundation really support both the current portal and your new colossus? And why is it strictly necessary to build three massive entrances, sir, for such a rustic part of town? (*Letters of Daan Goudsmit and Hans Donkerzijde*, 1622-23).

No matter for Donkerzijde. He brushed off the resignation of his assistant of twenty years' standing without remorse, and pressed on.

Workmen were often baffled by what it was exactly Donkerzijde intended to build. One workman thought the final blueprint was only a hasty sketch, and ate his lunch off of it. Donkerzijde now sorely lacked a draftsman who could translate his grandiose vision of triangular arches, gables, gryphon, and pentagrams into hard specifications. Morale was low, and as the boss was often off-site, laborers often deserted their tasks for their casks of beer or pipes. Speculation about Donkerzijde's sanity was the chief topic of conversation (van den Brink, 172).

Even after building began, Donkerzijde was not averse to changing his mind or adding features. Last minute design changes inevitably led to cost overruns, and soon the budget of forty thousand guilders had been spent without a single brick having been laid. Donkerzijde's explanations to the city fathers now fell on death ears. But with the Muiderpoort area now a disturbing aggregation of building materials, makeshift housing for laborers, and other bric-a-brac, building continued apace.

Working on draining the foundation was nearly complete when he decided that the perimeter must be pentagonal, much like the Vatican's fortress, the Castle St. Angelo. The digging of the pentagonal canal soon led to a breach. Water flowed into the soft land threatening the whole site, even the existing portal. Pumps were brought in, and a team of laborers (flippantly dubbed the first pumping brigade ("Eerste Pomp Divisie" or "EPD") by Donkerzijde) were given the famous order to "Pump or drown."

In 1672, the trade network of the Dutch Republic was still the envy of Europe. Louis XIV intended to humiliate the United Provinces, and Colbert wanted to take over the Dutch trade. The unusual alliance of France, England, and the bishoprics of Münster and Cologne temporarily deranged the European balance of power, and led to invasion of the Dutch Republic on three sides. The extreme measure of flooding the country was taken to stop the rapid inroads of the French army onto Dutch soil.

To some people the debacle seemed like God's punishment for Holland's material extravagance. Perhaps building projects like Donkerzijde's Muiderpoort were just what was wrong with Dutch society? The project was cancelled and Donkerzijde was financially liable for removing the material that still lay there. The *Plantage*'s grand future was revealed to be an illusion.

Donkerzijde was shattered by the failure to realize his portal, but through his GDG connections he secured a string of minor commissions (designing elaborate pissoirs for country estates along the Vecht) until his death in 1678.

He remained convinced that future generations would finally recognize his genius, and build his masterpiece from his original designs. He proved only partly right. In 1769, the original Muiderpoort began to sink on its own accord, and the decision was taken to rebuild. Work began on the second Muiderpoort, the one that exists to this day. While the architects reviewed and ultimately rejected his design, a jewel of Amsterdam architecture was finally achieved on the site of Donkerzijde's grandiose, but never realized, portal.

Sources

van den Brink, Jaap ed., *Encyclopedia of Minor Dutch Architects*. Amsterdam: Eloquent Publications, 2005

de Groot, Wim, *Letters of Daan Goudsmit and Hans Donkerzijde* (Volume III). Amsterdam: Aries Press, 2001

Boulanger, Francois, *Secret Societies in Amsterdam: 1621-1666*. London: GDG Press, 1981.

van Utrecht, Herman, *The Rise of International Banking in the Dutch Golden Age*. New York, New World Publications, 2004

Last Interview with the Zen Master

Shunryu Yamamoto ('JA-MAH-'MOH-TOH) was one of the earliest and most influential proponents of Zen Buddhism in the United States. Arriving in Los Angeles in June, 1963 he established a Zen monastery and gained a faithful American following.

In February 1972 Yamamoto died in a bizarre accident at the Burbank Invitational Dart Championship. Thousands mourned his death. He had done much to shape the American style of Zen Buddhism.

Yamamoto's brand of Zen Buddhism stressed the complete absurdity of life, and the futility of reason in comprehending it. Instead, he always advised his followers to "follow the Inner Voice." He always resisted universal moral codes. For Yamamoto, "the only constant in life is change," and he urged his disciples to constantly adapt to new situations. For a short time Yamamoto was a countercultural icon, and was widely sought out by the media, members of which he always treated with the greatest courtesy.

Unfortunately, he left behind no writings, "not even a laundry list" according to his grieved lifelong confidante, whom he called Baka ('BA KA). Students of Yamamoto are forced to rely on transcriptions of his utterances, and the unreliable memories of his followers. Some have even claimed that he penned the famous 1960s slogan "Make Love, Not War," but this is unconfirmed by his biographers.

Thus, Yamamoto's disciples still treasure his December 1971 interview with John Milner of LADIES MAN magazine, which would prove to be the last of his life.

Beverly Hills—On Saturday, I interviewed Shunryu Yamamoto in his large condominium two blocks off Rodeo Drive. His confidante, Baka, answered the door, and led me through Yamamoto's plush quarters, which featured an enormous kitchen, full dining room, and TV room. Baka offered me a Poptart and after I refused he led me down a long hallway to a small bedroom, where we found the Zen master applying paste to the walls.

Yamamoto performed even this humble task with skill and grace. Evidently he was wallpapering the room. Each of the three finished walls featured a different design. The room was in a state of disarray: dirty clothes, cheeseburger wrappers, full ashtrays, books and official documents littered the floor.

After a few words of greeting I believed myself to be in the presence of an extraordinary being. He radiated warmth and kindness. His face was so full of life and his soft bald head was reassuring in a strange way. Yamamoto spoke very slowly. He urged that we sit on the floor and the interview began.

Ladies Man: Master Yamamoto. This country has seen a rapidly growing interest in Zen Buddhism in the last five or ten years. Do you think this is a positive development, and to what degree do you feel responsible for this?
Yamamoto: America needs Zen very much. America needs Zen more than Zen needs America. Look around you. This country has no heart anymore. It is like an empty cup. Full of emptiness, and empty of fullness.

Its fullness is a bad fullness; an emptiness. America is full of emptiness, because it is too full of fullness. It is even empty of emptiness—but in the bad way.

I do not give myself much credit for popularizing Zen in America. It was inevitable anyway. I take credit for nothing. I am just an old man.
Ladies Man: Yet your followers, some of whom hold positions of considerable influence in this country, credit you for their success in life. Some have even donated large sums of money to your Zen Empowerment Temples. Do you see no tension between spiritual and monetary endeavors?
Yamamoto: For some men, making money is the only spiritual path worth following. One must always follow the Inner Voice....A few years back I had an investment banker who came to me seeking wisdom.

He said to me: "Yamamoto, Perfect Being. Simply tell me to give my money away and I will do it. I am unhappy. Money means nothing to me."

So I said to him: "Listen. Sit quietly. When I return, tell me what you have heard." So I left him alone and went to run a few errands.

When I returned I asked him: "And what did you hear, my son?" He said: "Nothing." And I said to him: "You see? When you are at peace, there is nothing. This is the highest lesson."

He had gained wisdom. He is now happier and richer than ever.

Ladies Man: Yet many critics of American culture, especially critics from abroad, point to America's craven materialism as evidence of its spiritual emptiness. You yourself just said that America was 'full of emptiness.' Why is it that the pursuit of wealth is bad for some men, yet enriching for others?

Yamamoto: All depends on the Inner Voice, which speaks differently to all men. Some men speak of the nobility of poverty. They become saints. This is what The Voice tells them to do. Other men: they think: "I would like a nice Italian automobile." Both men are correct. An old Zen parable treats this very thing.

One day a strong man sees a big rock. Every day he tries to lift the big rock. Every day he tries harder and harder, straining all his muscles, but the rock doesn't move. One day he gets the rock to budge a little. The next day a little more. And so on.

One day he picks the rock right over his head. But it slips and smashes him. Just like bug. No more lifting for him. You see?

Ladies Man: Are you saying that what we strive to do becomes our undoing?

Yamamoto: Yes and no. Some men desire nothing, and they are happy. Other men want to conquer the world. If they don't, it only makes them sick.

Ladies Man: I'm afraid I still don't understand. What do you teach at your Zen Empowerment Centers?

Yamamoto: Breathing. Breathing is very important.

When I first came to California a young man came to me for guidance. He believed he had read a great deal of Zen literature. He even believed he was ready to become a master himself. I told him that first he must breathe.

For a while he didn't understand, even though I sat him in a corner, and showed him proper *zazen* posture. He protested the simplicity of my lesson, but it is forbidden for a student to challenge his master. A few weeks later, he came up to me as I was leaving our swimming pool. He said: "Master Yamamoto. Why do you leave me sitting in the corner for weeks? Breathing is not so interesting. You do not understand. I am a scholar!"

He was a proud young man. So I grabbed him by the neck and shoved his face into the swimming pool. I held it there and counted to 200. He did not resist. When I released him his face was quite blue. When he regained his breath, he bowed, and left without a word.

He had learned breathing, the highest lesson.

Ladies Man: (*concealing his shock*) Aside from breathing: every Zen master stresses different aspects of Zen. Some stress Enlightenment, others stress living humbly and gracefully in this life. Your critics have noted that you seem to lack core beliefs. Can't you summarize your essential teachings for our readers?

Yamamoto: It is impossible to talk about my beliefs in detail. I have no beliefs; this is Zen. The more we read; the stupider we become. The more we think; the farther from the truth we go. It is like this: *A man drinks a cup of tea.*

Ladies Man: And?

Yamamoto: That is it. *A man drinks a cup of tea.* That is everything; the highest lesson. Simply be. Simply do.

Ladies Man: It is said that you do not place a lot of stock in Western rationality to solve man's problems. Do you utilize *koans* [Zen riddles] to illustrate the futility of reason?

Yamamoto: Yes, I find *koans* useful, especially with proud intellectuals.

Ladies Man: Do you have any favorite *koans*?

Yamamoto: Yes. One goes like this: *"What is there nothing of?"*

Ladies Man: I don't know.

Yamamoto: Exactly.

Ladies Man: Many other holy men have also displayed astonishing wisdom and knowledge at a young age. Did you receive any special training? Did you have a learned master? Are you well read in Classical Zen literature?

Yamamoto: No....No....Yes.

Ladies Man: Could you elaborate?

Yamamoto: I discovered the cosmic order of things when I was three years old. I remember it well. My father, who was a simple rice farmer, was beating my mother with a large sack of wheat. Even as a child I knew this was Zen. Even then I understood everything—except where he got that sack of wheat.

Later that night, my mother, the kindest woman I have ever known, stabbed him in the leg with a bread knife; I knew that this too was Zen. I understood everything....My father never wanted me to become a Zen master. But there was an old man in our village. We gave him a crude nickname, which could be translated as: 'man who should be tossed into the deep ocean.' He was not liked, this man. But one day he said to me: "Yamamoto, Almost Perfect Being, life is like waking up, to find that you are dreaming, that you are awake, but want to sleep." After that, I understood everything. I had no need of training. I learned the highest lesson.

Ladies Man: And what about Zen literature? Have you written anything yourself?

Yamamoto: Yes, I have read the Zen classics. They are of no value whatsoever, and so are very good. So full of Zen....I once wrote a poem about Zen, and showed it to the great Zen poet, Yamaguchi. He said to me: Yamamoto, Almost Perfect Being, this is the last poem to be written. The greatest poem. After this, we have no more need for Zen literature ever again. Learn it until you know it better than your own name. Then place it on a fire, and shout it to your whole village. It is the greatest poem in our tradition, and must never be seen on mere paper!"

Ladies Man: Would you mind sharing it with our readers?

Yamamoto: I forgot it completely. A long time ago. That was what Yamaguchi was trying to teach me: that forgetting is the secret to life. He burnt it himself then and there, before I had even learned it by heart or shouted it to anyone. But the lesson I do remember: To live a Zenful life, you must forget everything, let go of everything. This is the highest lesson.

Ladies Man: Yet Yamaguchi's poetry books sell by the thousands in Japan, and he himself continues writing volumes of poetry. Do you see no contradiction in his teaching?

Yamamoto: No. This too is Zen.

Ladies Man: Don't you feel we should develop our artistic gifts?

Yamamoto: Not necessarily. Take my friend, Baka. He comes from my village. We were friends even as boys. Baka was always a gifted pianist, praised in all of Japan even as a child. But he became too proud of his gift.

One day when we were young men he came to me for advice. Even then I was regarded as a wise man. He said to me: "Yamamoto, Almost Perfect Being, what should I do with my life?"

I said: "Baka. You love the piano more than your own life. Artistic pride is corroding your mind. You need to reconnect to the life-forces. You like to work with your hands. You should become a baker. Bake, Baka, bake!"

And so he went off to baking school. Soon he lost three fingers in blender. You see?

Ladies Man: You mean you—

Yamamoto: No more piano for Baka.

Ladies Man: Zen Buddhists believe in a vast diversity of practices. Many swear by sitting in the lotus position and meditating. Others believe in the sacred tea ceremony. Still others believe that it is the "Zen mindset" that is important, that one should realize their "oneness with the world" regardless of the task. Are there any specific practices that you believe to be the most effective?

Yamamoto: The practices you speak of are all mere exercises. I encourage my own students to listen to their own minds; the mind will always tell you what you should do. This is the highest lesson.

Ladies Man: So what meditative practices have your students followed?

Yamamoto: One man believed he could achieve *satori* ["*enlightenment*"] simply by sitting quietly and drinking thirty cups of black coffee every evening. He died. Pancreatic cancer. A pity. Another man walked over hot coals in his bare feet and experienced great pain. It was sad.

Others have better success with the tea ceremony, or just sitting. This is what I do. I sit. Sometimes I wallpaper. (*Gestures to the walls with his pasty fingers.*)

It doesn't matter. Little Baka watches television. All day. "Gomer Pyle," I think....So you see, for every man there is a path.

Ladies Man: Biographical information about you is still somewhat sketchy. What about the women in your life? What jobs have you held?

Yamamoto: My second wife was always my favorite. I had a special nickname for her. In English it could be translated as: "Everything is swallowed by large fish." She was delightful. A most graceful being. All three of my wives died very young. It is tragic.

I've worked many jobs in my life. I was trained to be rice farmer. Like my father. But I always hated rice. It sticks to my teeth And it was all we ever ate.

As a young man I moved to Kyoto. Here I shined shoes, washed dishes. Many other jobs. Then I joined the army. World War II.

I remember now that many of my comrades were trying to kill our Captain, Captain Mifune. A hard man. Made us eat sand. One night four men threw grenades into his quarters. Only two exploded. Killed his mistress and his cat, but the captain himself was unharmed. He caught the traitors immediately. Tied them up for execution.

Then he summoned me. He says to me: "Yamamoto, Almost Perfect Being, I don't like you. But you are very wise for a rotten, young sapling. We are at war, Yamamoto, Almost Perfect Being. We need men. What should I do?"

So I looked at him, much as I look at you now, and say: "Captain Mifune, Pride of the Japanese Army, these men are villainous traitors. Worse than the lowest reptiles. But save our precious bullets. Give each man one rolling pin, and make them beat each other to the death. But for his endurance, promote the winner one rank."

And so they fought brutally for hours. But that is how my little Baka became a second lieutenant.

After the war I begged for food for many years. Spent some time in India. Then I came to America.

Ladies Man: But surely—

Yamamoto: Very fierce with a rolling pin, that Baka....Just like samurai. But no more baking for him.

Ladies Man: Now forgive me for asking this, Master Yamamoto, but—"

Yamamoto: But I already know what you want to ask.

Ladies Man: Well, then how do you respond?

Yamamoto: Yes and no.

Ladies Man: Perhaps I should ask the question anyway, for the sake of our less psychic readers. Some people have also doubted your sincerity. The *Washington Post* recently wrote of you that: "Master Yamamoto dazzles rich and gullible Americans with his Zen bag of tricks. Revenues from his non-profit Zen Empowerment Temples enable him to lead the life of a pasha, couched in luxury in one of the finest condominiums in California, while he oversees a vast empire of temples, ashrams, and self-help literature written by other people." How do you respond to this?

Yamamoto: I own nothing. This is why I have everything. I own nothing. This apartment? Why, it belongs to Baka!

Ladies Man: But doesn't he work for you?

Yamamoto: Yes.

Ladies Man: And don't you pay him?

Yamamoto: You don't understand. It is like this. A man walks through the forest and discovers a sealed glass box. Inside the box he sees a string of the finest pearls. As he picks up the box to smash it on a rock, the box says to him: "Man. I am a box. Don't smash me on a rock. If you do, the pearls too shall be destroyed." But the man smashes the box anyway. You see?

Ladies Man: Frankly, no. Does he still get the pearls?

Yamamoto: You don't understand. It is like this: A man with no teeth goes to the dentist. The dentist begins to drill—

Ladies Man: Wait. What about the pearls?

Yamamoto: In Zen, there are no interpretations. No explanations. This is the highest lesson.

Baka appears in the doorway. He speaks in Japanese. Yamamoto nods and holds up his fingers in a V, a private gesture to which Baka replies by raising his stump of a hand.

Yamamoto: You must excuse me, Mr. Milner. I have an important phone call. We can finish some other time.

Yamamoto bowed and ended the interview. His death in late February, 1972 shocked the Zen community. Also calamitous was the fire in early March, 1972, which destroyed all of his personal documents. Baka still runs The Zen Empowerment Temples.

Reviews of Imaginary Movies

Disney Movies

Disney's *Genesis*

God – James Earl Jones
Adam – John Cusack
Eve – Cameron Diaz
The Serpent – Jim Carey
Noah – Morgan Freeman
Abraham – Danny Glover
Sarah – Oprah Winfrey
Jacob – Albert Brooks
Esau – Russell Crowe

———

Disney's *Genesis*, much like the book, is a fascinating hodge-podge of stories about fatherhood. Perhaps the main weakness of this adorable animated picture is the producers' attempt to inject their favorite rock classics into the soundtrack.

The opening scenes depict the creation of the world in fantastic bursts of color as God (James Earl Jones) commands "Let There Be Light!" Lush vegetation bursts forth (as in time-lapse photography nature shots). The beasts of the air and the field are soon roaming the earth in a global menagerie of animals that makes *The Lion King* seem pathetic in retrospect.

God Himself appears in the form of the Sun King, beaming at the adoration of His creatures. Thousands of mammals sing a moving rendition of The Beatles song "Here Comes the Sun."

God then creates Adam (John Cusack) and Eve (Cameron Diaz), who frolic in paradise for ten solid minutes, which seems like an eternity in a movie. We are waiting for something to happen. Strangely, Adam and Eve wear fig leaves from the very beginning (instead of *after* they have eaten the forbidden fruit, as in the book), but this avoids the problem of showing them naked. Instead, they hold hands, kiss like naughty children, and gallop through an open meadow, singing a variation of Meat Loaf's "Paradise by the Dashboard Light"—"Paradise by the Good Lord's Light."

The serpent (Jim Carey) soon steals the show by shape-shifting himself into a bizarre creature, a serpent with legs. He has also the ability to stick his tongue clear across a meadow to whisper in the ears of other animals and cause trouble. Soon he is slithering up to Eve and promising her that the forbidden fruit gives life everlasting. Eve eats the forbidden fruit with the Serpent to the tune of the Rolling Stones' "(I Can't Get No) Satisfaction."

Eve begs Adam to eat the fruit too. "It's *so good*," she moans. Adam looks turned on by this and eats the fruit hungrily. After Eve and Adam both have eaten the fruit, the soundtrack plays Aretha Franklin's "(You Make Me Feel Like) A Natural Woman" while we fade out. Just as they are wiping the fruit juice off their lips God emerges from the clouds to punish them.

This quick transition avoids the theological problems with the book's version of the story, where Adam and Eve run away and cover themselves with mere fig leaves to conceal their nudity from the supposedly all-seeing Creator of the universe (whose supernatural powers must surely include X-ray vision).

Adam is terrified that God will kill them for their sin (and considering the violence that God heaps on human beings throughout this movie, Adam has every right to be worried about God's temper). Instead, God just banishes Adam and Eve from Eden. They are relieved. The fields east of Eden look just as green and lush to us as Eden itself, so it's not so bad.

The next story in the book is Cain and Abel, but the creators of Disney's *Genesis* must have realized how unsuitable for children the Bible really is. Disturbing stories, such as Cain's shocking murder of Abel, are left on the cutting room floor. But this way we can go straight to the story of Noah's Ark, which plays more to Disney's obvious strengths.

The utter depravity of the human race in Noah's time is shown during a three minute montage of turpitude (while the Beatles' "Twist and Shout" plays in the background). Town dwellers bow down and worship shapeless piles of wood and rocks. Men leer at each other with unusual interest and consume incredible volumes of red meat and red wine.

When God (James Earl Jones) first tells Noah (Morgan Freeman) His great plan to destroy the entire world by flood and kill every living thing, we feel He is overreacting a bit. After all, God made Man imperfect, so drowning all the animals for the sins of Man seems unfair. But several flashbacks to scenes of human depravity are meant to convince even small children that God is fully justified in exterminating every sentient being on the planet— except for the chosen people and animals aboard Noah's ark.

The Great Flood sequences are spellbinding: water gushes into the dens of sin with pinpoint accuracy and carries off the wicked to water-soaked deaths. The only animals shown drowning are a few scurrilous donkeys and one very disgusting-looking pig that no one will ever miss.

Meanwhile, Noah's ark is filled with adorable animals, who look at each other with knowing smiles, glad to have escaped the fate of the rest of their species. However, logistical problems such as waste product removal for thousands of animals are never explained.

As the tide recedes, Noah and his family stand on the deck of the ark, as they get their first look at dry land while the soundtrack plays the Johnny Nash soft rock classic, "I Can See Clearly Now (the Rain is Gone)."

After Noah comes the story of Abraham and Sarah. Abraham and Sarah appear to be younger than 100 years old (as in the book). But God gives Abraham a blue pill anyway. Abraham disappears with aged Sarah into their tent, and before you know it Isaac is born. Thus, Abraham's concubines are completely omitted from the movie.

Soon an angel of the Lord appears to Abraham to tell him that he must sacrifice young Isaac on God's express orders. Abraham shrugs as if this is exactly what he would expect from a God who only recently destroyed the world by flood because of few people's victimless crimes. Abraham is prepared to do it (as Cat Stevens' "Father and Son" plays), but then the angel appears to say it was only a test. While we are supposed to be impressed by how reasonable God is, Abraham doesn't seem convinced; he only looks weary about God's absurd (in Kierkegaard's sense) ways.

The story of Isaac's sons, Jacob and Esau revolves around the Blessing of the Lord. Esau is the elder brother and therefore should get the Blessing automatically as his birthright. However, Jacob is wily. He connives to *steal* it from Esau by offering his starving brother a bowl of porridge (worth about $1) in exchange for the Blessing (worth millions of dollars, especially when including the compound interest).

But somehow stealing the Blessing once wasn't enough for Jacob, or maybe the Bible was sloppily edited, so we are given the even more ridiculous story of how Jacob steals the Blessing a second time. This time Jacob puts on a fur and goes to Isaac's deathbed. He convinces his blind father that he is the hairy eldest son and rightful heir, Esau. This is a trick right out of a Bugs Bunny cartoon, yet it works! Jacob (Israel) becomes the father of a great nation. Moral of the story: Honesty doesn't get you anywhere.

The destruction of Sodom and Gomorrah features spectacular animation, but we are not told why God destroyed these cities exactly (and so soon after destroying the whole world with the great flood too). By lashing out and killing his creatures so often, God seems more like a vindictive Zeus than the loving father figure that many people imagine.

Genesis is a very entertaining film, but a curious one for Disney to have commissioned. Even with some of the most bizarre scenes from the book left out of the film, God emerges as most erratic character. He appears out of the blue and heaps scathing physical punishment on people for seemingly trifling offenses.

The film also suffers from a lack of a central character (other than God) to unify the various stories. But the animation and the music are spectacular. The soundtrack, featuring a rousing rendition of "God Bless America" sung by the entire cast, is selling well in stores.

Disney's *King David*

King David – Brad Pitt
The Lord (Yahweh) – James Earl Jones
Saul – James Woods
Goliath – Hulk Hogan
Bathsheba – Salma Hayek
Michal – Cameron Diaz

Continuing its recent strategy of animating classical Bible stories, Disney's *King David* covers all the highlights of the Israelite hero's fabled career: his precocious lyre-playing, his slaying of the giant Philistine, Goliath; his assumption of the throne of Israel; and his impressive career of fornication.

Of course the background to the story of David is the story of King Saul. Before the time of Saul, Israel had no king and was ruled by the judges. "There was no king in Israel, and every man did what was right in his own eyes." The Israelites keep turning their backs on the Lord, worshipping idols at every opportunity. They neglect the Lord despite His generous assistance, such as free land, manna, and the extermination of the Israelites' enemies on all sides.

Curiously, God's hand-picked monarch is the hapless Saul, whom political science students may remember as the inspiration for divine-right monarchy theory. Yet Saul is an incompetent king, who fails to vanquish the Philistines, and even to keep those wayward Israelites happy and focused on the Lord.

Enter David, a handsome youth who plays the harp like a god, and who is loved by the Lord. The Lord inspires young David to fling a rock at the head of the previously invincible Goliath. The Israelites see that David is great. So why didn't the Lord just make David the king? Instead, years go by while David, the Lord, and all Israel wait for King Saul to finally die, or at least to step aside for the glorious David.

Instead, Saul tries to have David, his rival, killed. Saul sets a trap by promising his lubricious daughter, Michal, to David—on the unlikely condition that he can bring back the foreskins of 200 slain Philistines. Thanks to the Lord, David succeeds in bringing back the foreskins, surprising both Saul, as well as millions of movie-goers, who are shocked to hear the word "foreskin" uttered in a Disney movie—for the first time ever (subliminal messages aside).

King Saul is obviously hopelessly inept, and the movie quotes the Bible that even "the Lord repenteth" for having chosen Saul. Saul resembles the Nixon of 1973-1974, clinging to power despite universal opposition and loathing. The Lord won't even answer his prayers. The Lord has had enough of Saul. An old medium correctly predicts that Saul and his sons will die the following day, which they all do, prompting a massive celebration.

Finally, David is able to take command of the Israelites. David's first priority is to build up a vast harem, including Bathsheba, his favorite. David couples with the most delectable women from his harem so frequently—while still maintaining the Lord's favor—that traditional monogamy seems thoroughly Victorian and discredited. Even on his deathbed, David tries to invigorate himself by sleeping with several women from his harem. It does not save him, but it is a glorious effort nonetheless.

The death of King David is a time of mourning in Israel (the background animation seems lifted from *Bambi*) even with the reign of King Solomon on the horizon. David realized that the Blessing of the Lord really means "life more abundant": political power; good food and wine; the ecstasy of worship; music and poetry; and limitless concubines. David's rock-star life-style may make him seem like a pagan or even a Satanist to some true Christian believers, but Disney may have calculated that this is a declining demographic and that most Americans now embrace David's pagan values.

David is in many ways an ideal Disney protagonist. He is an action hero equipped with courage, good looks, and the Blessing of the Lord. He scores high in most audience focus groups, and he benefits from Americans' relative ignorance of his exploits other than the slaying of Goliath.

King David is a winner, an energetic entertainment, suitable for most children 10 years and up, depending on individual parents' feelings about the mass slaughter of innocents, eviscerated foreskins, random violence, and nubile harems.

Disney's *The Book of Revelations*

God – James Earl Jones
Bob (The Antichrist) – John Travolta
Satan – Richard Gere
King of Gog and Magog – Omar Sharif
King of the East – Chow Yun Fat
Luke the Itinerant Minister – Eddie Murphy
John the Prophet – Robin Williams

———

Although it was box-office poison, Disney's *Book of Revelations* has become a critical darling on DVD, ranking with *Fantasia* and *The Hunchback of Notre Dame* as sacred texts in the Disney canon. The lush animation softens the sometimes upsetting apocalyptic material for young viewers as they watch the rise of the Antichrist followed by Satan's world domination.

After the opening credits, an old prophet named John (Robin Williams) sleeps under a tree and has an extraordinary dream. It is the End Time, and the people of the world indulge in sinful pleasures. We see a Paris-like metropolis teeming with rich people, who whip their slaves around crowded marketplaces and force them to carry their large shopping packages. A DVD freeze-frame even reveals that many of the wicked are buying Bugs Bunny stuffed animals and other merchandise of Disney arch-rival Time Warner.

The metropolis is saturated with video screens from which the Antichrist (John Travolta), a dynamic leader known only as "Bob," commands the people to work harder so that they can shop more. Bob tricks most people into accepting a "mark" on their right hands (a yellow star, but up close it looks like a UPC barcode) in exchange for more credit at the shopping malls.

From heaven, God (James Earl Jones) is enraged watching the people line up to take the mark of Bob. His angels prepare plagues: blood-soaked rivers, skin boils, the death of 1/3 of all living things on earth, and a specially prepared "Lake of Fire and Brimstone."

The good people of the earth see the plagues and are quick to spot God's anger. Led by an itinerant minister, Luke (Eddie Murphy), they repent and ascend into heaven in a stately procession to the tune of Blondie's epoch-making pop hit "Rapture." Luke admittedly is not a character in the book, but is popular with some demographic groups.

Meanwhile the wicked people, even after seeing the good people rise to heaven, the rivers turn to blood, and the sun eclipsed for weeks, are still too pig-headed to repent for having taken the mark of Bob. They simply resume their shopping. One may wonder how the wicked were smart enough to get rich and rule the world in the first place when they are too dense to know that they face imminent annihilation at the hands of the all-loving God.

Bob himself is soon wounded by one of God's lightning bolts, but he is revived by Satan (Richard Gere) and resumes his evil ways. Bob announces from the TV screens that he will soon be invading the tiny, desolate valley of Armageddon in ancient Palestine, in order to "protect its human rights."

Bob and Satan lead their troops into battle singing the rousing song "A Fight, Tonight," set to the tune of *West Side Story's* 'Tonight.' Their opponents are the King of Gog and Magog (Omar Sharif), and the King of the East (Chow Yun Fat) in the greatest battle in human history. The battle scenes feature some of the most spectacular animation ever produced. Watching the wicked destroy each other in a triangular exchange of tactical nuclear weapons will warm the souls of true believers everywhere.

God finally enters the battle with a giant sword, with which he stabs the wicked and burns them over the Lake of Fire and Brimstone, almost as if working a barbecue. Finally, he tosses Bob and Satan himself into the Lake without much effort. Unfortunately, this scene may prompt awkward questions from children such as: why didn't God simply destroy Satan at the dawn of time, and thereby prevent thousands of years of human suffering?

No matter. Now the angels open up tombs all over the world so that the dead can ascend into heaven for the Last Judgment. Some remain in heaven with God. The rest are tossed into the Lake of Fire and Brimstone, experiencing only two minutes of consciousness before being plunged into eternal punishment without even a cup of coffee. And there they will stay for all eternity—God's much-vaunted mercy notwithstanding.

Then God turns his attention to destroying the earth. Because the last time He destroyed nearly all living creatures—during the time of Noah—He had promised not to use the terrible method of flooding, this time God uses fire to incinerate the earth and all its creatures instead.

God then creates a new earth; one with streets of gold that lead to the capital city, which Disney-haters might point out resembles the Magic Kingdom itself. The people live in eternal bliss, with multitudes singing a rousing rendition of Beethoven's "Ode to Joy" on numerous occasions.

Finally, John the prophet wakes up back on his island in 1st century Greece. And now we know: It was all a dream. John awakens on a stormy morning and writes down his dream. What a relief! The end.

Many rumors still surround Disney's bizarre decision to make and release *Revelations*. Aside from the highly disturbing subject matter itself, the message of *Revelations* seems uncharacteristic to long-term students of Disney. The vision of the righteous poor ascending into heaven while the evil rich endure God's punishment seems dangerously close to a critique of market capitalism. What could be wrong with shopping?

And the final scene showing the new earth with streets of gold seems suspiciously communal, as if God has redistributed wealth. Some Christians have suggested that Disney makes Satanic propaganda (as seen by the endless parade of magicians, witches, sorcerers in the Disney canon), or at least to hide subliminal sexual imagery in the animation. But instead, *Revelations* is a film that clearly sides with God. Strange.

One Disney story editor reputedly suggested inverting the class identities—to portray the poor as the wicked, and the rich as the righteous. But Disney decided that such a stark reversal of the usual Christian revenge-fantasy would upset viewers, even affluent ones, so they chose a safer course.

Since the original Biblical text is so ragged and hallucinatory, the Disney script-doctors wisely focus on the central good vs. evil plot, and punch up the text's lack of clear narrative thread. Although not a box-office champion, *Revelations* has new life on DVD. Strong sales of *Revelations* merchandise continue, including action-figures of the major characters: the Antichrist, Satan, and the King of Gog and Magog (Russia), who has been very popular due to his uncanny resemblance to Boba Fett from the *Star Wars* movies.

Disney's *Animal Farm*

Voice of Snowball – Tom Hanks
Voice of Napoleon – Danny De Vito

This animated adaptation of George Orwell's anti-totalitarian novel rejects unmarketable political allegory in favor of idyllic scenes of animal harmony.

In order to make the story more palatable for children, the script deviates from the book's political message in several critical ways. The novel's violent animal uprising against Farmer Jones (symbolic of the Bolshevik Revolution) is whitewashed into the movie's voluntary "vacation" for Farmer Jones. In an improbable scene, Farmer Jones (carrying a suitcase, wearing a Hawaiian shirt and shades) *appoints* Snowball the pig (the novel's Trotsky character) as leader in his absence. "Keep an eye on things, Snowy," he helpfully advises Snowball.

Although the pigs do put the other animals to work (they sing the catchy tune "Work Is Freedom," a clear echo of "Whistle While You Work"), the pig's dream of a Workers' Utopia is eventually realized through the introduction of adorable, doe-eyed agricultural robots. These "AgriBots" (another blockbuster merchandising opportunity for Disney) are themselves given to frequent song, such as the catchy "Napoleon's Got Semolians Now." They dramatically boost crop yields and enable the pigs and the other animals to live a life of lemonade-sipping leisure.

The novel's protracted power struggle between Napoleon and Snowball (symbolizing Stalin and Trotsky) is reduced to the film's climactic Hot Dog Eating Contest. Here the two overstuffed pigs eventually declare a draw and embrace each other to the sounds of hearty belching. The other animals cheer, celebrating the hard-wrought bounty of the land. Even the AgriBots pause from their work to look upon this final celebration, their eyes filled with an almost organic satisfaction.

Although readers of the book may be put off by the evisceration of Orwell's message (the farm is called Kargill Farms), rollicking songs such as "Two is Better Than Four," "Snowball in Heaven's Chance," and "Work is Freedom" make it a good time for the kids—whose future reading of the book will forever be overdetermined by the indelible images of Disney animation.

Disney's *1984*

Winston Smith – George Clooney
Julia – Julia Roberts
Big Brother – Al Pacino
O'Brien – Anthony Hopkins
Goldstein – Steven Spielberg
Thought Police – Carrie Fisher

A quick look at your newspaper's movie section may confirm your suspicion that Hollywood's store of compelling ideas is bankrupt. This might explain Disney's recent tactic of producing animated musical versions of classic

George Orwell novels (see Disney's *Animal Farm* above)—all, supposedly, with the "magic Disney touch." Unfortunately, in these movies, that magic touch consists largely of adapting classic pop songs for the film's soundtrack in order to please Boomer-parents in the audience.

Hence, Disney's *1984* opens with the familiar clarinet notes of the Beatles' classic "When I'm Sixty-Four," but the lyrics have been revamped into the more sinister "Will They Deceive Me? / Will They Believe Me? / In Nineteen Eighty-Four!"

Disney's *1984* stars George Clooney as Winston Smith, an information worker in the Party, which rules the futuristic superstate of Oceania. He attends political rallies, where large Telescreens project images of Big Brother (Al Pacino), while the crowds chant with adoration at their leader. Big Brother's theme song, played whenever he appears, is "He Ain't Heavy, He's Big Brother," a variation of the soft-rock classic "(He Ain't Heavy) He's My Brother." But unlike in the novel, the rallies are not seen as sinister events. People are even issued ration tickets for Victory Gin as token payment for appearing in the crowd. People are paid to watch the Telescreens.

Unfortunately, the filmmakers fail to establish a consistent tone for the movie. At first the cloudy gray animation seems appropriate for Orwell's dark vision. But the steady procession of spritely musical numbers clashes with the animation, creating cognitive dissonance. We are uncertain how to respond to this material. Big Brother, so often the object of song ("Big Brother and Big Sister," "Atom Heart Brother"), seems more like a benevolent despot or Oz figure than a totalitarian dictator.

We are also slightly distracted by the many Hollywood in-jokes, as the film pokes fun at Disney's arch-rivals in the mass entertainment industry and even at Disney itself. Ultimately, Disney's *1984* works in as a baroque satire of contemporary entertainment.

As in the novel, Winston Smith's occupation (information worker) is to doctor old newspapers and books to ensure that they are consistent with the Party's current policies. Winston's task is to delete all references to "Unpersons"—persons that Big Brother has decided should be expunged from the nation's consciousness forever. In a dig at Disney's arch-rival Time-Warner, Winston is shown sitting at his computer methodically deleting every existing picture of Ted Turner (Vice President at Time-Warner), Jane Fonda (shown as her 1968 sex-kitten *Barbarella*), and Rupert Murdoch.

Winston leads a dull life in service of the Party, until one day a woman Julia (Julia Roberts) bumps into him on the street and passes him a note which reads "I love you." This act is in open defiance of the Party, which forbids love and marriage, and permits coupling only for the purpose of procreation. (Any children are immediately handed over to the loving care of Big Brother.) But despite the Telescreens watching them from every angle,

Winston and Julia hold hands, skipping down the streets of Air Strip One (Britain) to the tune of The Partridge Family's hit "I Think I Love You."

Julia soon hands Winston the banned writings of the notorious enemy of the state, Goldstein (Steven Spielberg), who encourages resistance to Big Brother. Winston is terrified to possess such contraband material, and fears that he will end up in the hands of the Thought Police. If you look carefully, you will see that the "contraband literature" is the screenplay for the movie *1941*, a rare 1980 Spielberg directorial embarrassment.

The bizarre helmets worn by the Thought Police—although superficially an attempt to parody Princess Leia's dual crescent-roll hairstyle in *Star Wars* (Carrie Fisher is even the voice of the first Thought Policeman we see)—bear an uncanny similarity to Disney's own mouse ears logo. Thus, the images of legions of Thought Police patrolling the streets of Oceania, wearing what appear to be mouse ear helmets, elicit unintentional nervous laughter as we reflect upon Disney's control of our children's minds.

During a three-minute montage we watch children turning in their parents to the Thought Police for "thought crimes," while the soundtrack blares "The Thought Police" to the tune of the old Cheap Trick song "The Dream Police." We are unsure whether to laugh or be nervous, and so we just look apprehensively at the many children in the audience, who we know often obediently log on to Disney-controlled web sites, thereby volunteering their parents' web history and purchasing patterns.

Soon the Thought Police hand over Winston and Julia to O'Brien (Anthony Hopkins), the High Party Official, for punishment for their thought crimes and extra-Party love. O'Brien knows from surveillance that Winston's greatest fear is rats. So Winston and Julia are tied down to a bed while numerous rats crawl over them to the tune of "The Rats in the Cradle (and They'll Kill You Soon)" a variation of Harry Chapin's "The Cat's in the Cradle (and the Silver Spoon)." Again, as the rats look like Mickey Mouse's first cousins, we wonder how much of the anti-Disney fun is sanctioned, and how much the director snuck past an unusually dim-witted Disney censor.

Luckily for Winston and Julia, the rats gnaw away their ropes, allowing them to escape from the heavily-fortified Ministry of Truth compound. But soon they are hunted down by tanks, helicopters, and armored personnel carriers. They climb to the top of London's Big Ben, and decide to leap off and die rather than face further torture by the Thought Police.

As they are falling, Winston wakes up in his own bed, and we realize it was all a dream.

Winston then walks out of his Manhattan apartment to Times Square, where the gargantuan video screens saturate his vision with the brand names of the world's great corporations. "We are not controlled only because the Telescreens constantly look upon us," muses Winston in the film's final line. "We are controlled because we look upon the Telescreens."

The Movies of Jake Steiger

Beginning with his first film, *Mr. Kleen*, writer/director Jake Steiger made some of the most popular films of the 1980s and 1990s.

Steiger's Filmography
Mr. Kleen
Meet the Gambinos
Bringing up Eight
Serial Murderers Naturally
Ford
The Lusitania

Mr. Kleen

Mickey Kleen – Arnold Schwarzenegger
Toshiro – Harvey Keitel
Written and directed by Jake Steiger

――――

Jake Steiger's directorial debut starred Arnold Schwarzenegger as a mentally unbalanced janitor working at the Sears Tower in Chicago. One day a Japanese terrorist group led by Toshiro (a masked Harvey Keitel) violently seizes the tallest building in the world and demands $25 million to not blow it up. Despite the quick response of the police, army, and National Guard, the building seems doomed until Mickey Kleen (Schwarzenegger), ready to clock out for the day, spots some broken glass on the floor.

Mindful of his solemn duty to keep the floors clean, Mickey grabs his mop and starts following a long trail of blood and broken glass. Soon he stumbles upon some of Keitel's terrorists. He easily beats them up with his mop and takes their semi-automatic weapons. As he mops up their blood, Mickey suffers from some heavy-handed Freudian flashbacks about his sloppy, long-lost father, who always made Mickey mop up after his alcoholic vomiting. Audiences witness the spectacle of Arnold Schwarzenegger nearly in tears.

As he works his way through the building, dispatching legions of Japanese terrorists, Mickey seems more concerned with the state of the building he has maintained (single-handedly?) for so long than with the ceaseless violence in which he is embroiled.

Mickey's janitorial skills come in handy as he creates lethal explosives from familiar household chemicals, such as floor cleaners and detergents. Product placement in this movie is in extremely bad taste.

Eventually he dispatches Keitel himself by spraying liquid detergent into his eyes. The ink on Keitel's mask begins to run, and Mickey peels off the mask, discovering that Keitel is his long-lost father disguised as a Japanese terrorist. Mickey's psychological wounds are healed by seeing his father, who, blinded by the detergent, is unable to recognize his son as the police carry him away. There are strong suggestions of a sequel.

In interviews, Steiger pointed out that, despite the non-stop violence and $55 million dollars in property damage, not a single character actually dies on screen in *Mr. Kleen*, showing Steiger's unusual restraint and social responsibility as an action-movie director.

Meet the Gambinos

Sammy Carlotti – Robert De Niro
Maury Yablonovich – Billy Crystal
Joey – Mickey Rourke
Sal – Joe Pesci
Don Salvatore Gambino – Burt Young
Crazy Frankie Sciotti – Danny DeVito
Tamar – Marisa Tomei
Written and directed by Jake Steiger

———

After the success of *Mr. Kleen*, Steiger turned to the crime genre, writing and directing *Meet the Gambinos*. Robert De Niro, on loan from director Martin Scorsese, stars as Sammy Carlotti, a humble Gambino Family hit man, wrongfully accused of defecting to the rival Castellano Family.

One day while using the toilet in a Little Italy bakery, Sammy overhears two of his closest colleagues arguing about the best way to kill Sammy for betraying the Family. Joey (Mickey Rourke) favors shooting him in the head and dumping him in the East River, but Sal (Joe Pesci) favors strangling him with a garrote and leaving his corpse in Central Park as a warning to would-be traitors. Meanwhile, Sammy must sit quietly on the toilet (apparently holding back anal eruptions) while they violently debate how to kill him for several suspenseful moments. Eventually they leave.

The next day Sammy launches a pre-emptive strike by sending Joey and Sal a tray of red peppers stuffed with plastic explosives. "How's that for heartburn!" Sammy quips later, watching Joey and Sal explode through a set of binoculars.

Now Sammy is on the run from the Gambinos, who in this movie seem to control the entire New York City Police Department. To disguise himself, Sammy adopts the garb of a Hasidic Jew. While walking around Crown Heights he meets a liberal rabbi named Maury Yablonovich (Billy Crystal), whose mincing way of speaking provides a comic interlude in the midst of the general bloodbath. Maury doubts Sammy's story of being a rabbi. Eventually Sammy confides to Maury that he's running from the Gambinos. Maury believes Sammy is innocent of treachery; and if he ever clears his name with the Gambinos he plans to set Sammy up with his beautiful younger sister, Tamar (Marisa Tomei).

Soon the Gambinos find Sammy and bring him and hapless Maury (now also accused of being a Castellano hit man) back to Family headquarters for a show-trial for "crimes against the Family." The trial is held in an elaborate underground courtroom, with Don Salvatore Gambino (Burt Young) serving as judge (he even wears a robe and wig and bangs a gavel). Don Gambino solemnly pronounces both Sammy and Maury guilty of treason, "the most serious of all crimes against the Family."

Sammy protests his innocence, and begs the court spare his life in light of his many devoted years of gangland killing. Don Gambino is momentarily moved by Sammy's protestations of loyalty, but eventually dismisses him with the single word: *morte*.

Maury is bound and gagged, and placed on the Gambino yacht bound for Spain to die after a one-time stint as a sacrificial matador (a favor for a friendly Spanish crime syndicate).

Meanwhile, Sammy is placed in a bizarre-looking torture chamber, designed by Crazy Frankie Sciotti (Danny DeVito), the Gambinos' torturer-in-chief. Despite experiencing inhuman degrees of pain, Sammy survives, finally managing to free his hands and shove Sciotti's untucked shirttails into the cogs of his own infernal torture-chamber, pulling him in and grinding him to bits.

Sammy soon escapes from Gambino headquarters through a poorly guarded air-duct, hijacks a helicopter, and manages to overtake the Gambino yacht in the Atlantic, still carrying Maury on board. In the climactic shoot-out, Sammy kills everyone on board the yacht except Maury.

The movie then flashes forward a few years, when Sammy marries Maury's sister, Tamar. By marrying Tamar, Sammy has finally joined Maury's family, clearly a gentler family than the Gambinos.

Bringing up Eight

Phillip Stein – Marlon Brando
Ruth Stein – Meryl Streep
Jack Stein – Macaulay Culkin

Written, produced and directed by Jake Steiger

After directing two very profitable movies, Steiger spent nearly three years and $75 million dollars creating this thinly veiled autobiographical fable of his early life in Brighton Beach, New York. Macaulay Culkin stars as young Jack, a sensitive, misunderstood teenager, who enjoys making home movies of himself and his seven siblings. Marlon Brando co-stars as his gluttonous father, given to semi-intelligible mumblings and odd facial expressions. Meryl Streep is improbably cast as his histrionic mother, continuously protesting the loss of her youth to another (presumably unwanted) pregnancy.

The movie is shot as a period piece, with scenes of 1950s Manhattan and Brooklyn. Steiger refused to use stock footage of the city on "artistic grounds" and built elaborate sets on location in midtown Manhattan at staggering cost.

These provide the backdrop for Steiger's coming-of-age story. We see Jack fall in love, quit college, get his first job as a production assistant on a TV commercial, and experience other youthful milestones on his way to becoming a great Hollywood writer/director. Critics found it self-indulgent.

Marlon Brando, though paid $1 million dollars per day of shooting, very often forgot his lines and lapsed into unintelligible evocations of his past roles in *A Streetcar Named Desire*, *On the Waterfront*, and *The Godfather*.

Steiger later complained publicly that Brando had "never read the script" and "often made up his lines from scratch." Brando often called the Meryl Streep character "Stella!" (despite the fact that her character's name was Ruth), which caused delays to the filming at incalculable cost. Steiger later estimated that 80% of Brando's performance ended up on the cutting-room floor as "completely inappropriate gibberish." He resorted to the extreme measure of dubbing another actor's voice over Brando's—not always seamlessly—in order to salvage key scenes.

Steiger's movie about eight children raised by an unresponsive and egomaniacal Brooklyn father received poor critical reviews and box-office draw. Many critics were confused by the lack of story, writing off *Bringing Up Eight* as a "$75 million dollar home movie." Steiger invested and lost $10 million dollars of his own money on *Bringing Up Eight*, and many were claiming that his greatest work was already behind him.

Serial Murderers Naturally

Yank Feller – Kevin Costner
Luscious Wilson – Sharon Stone
Written, produced, and directed by Jake Steiger

With Universal Studios deserting him after *Bringing Up Eight* bombed at the box-office, Steiger was tentatively embraced by Time Warner, on the condition he return to action movies, his proven *métier*. Steiger—humbled and impoverished by *Bringing Up Eight*—responded obediently, producing, writing, and directing *Serial Murderers Naturally*, a 150 minute bloodbath that he later defended as a satire of the media's lust for violent news stories.

The movie opens with Yank Feller (Kevin Costner) being released from Rikers Island prison for a bank robbery he didn't commit. Because the bank robbery had received such intense publicity many years before, Yank must run a gauntlet of television cameras to fight his way to the waiting pink Cadillac convertible of his old flame, Luscious Wilson (Sharon Stone).

For the first ten minutes of the movie, Yank seems determined to walk a straight-and-narrow path. But when Luscious confesses that they have no money and no place to stay, Yank agrees to her scheme of robbing a Wal-Mart.

It is supposed to be a simple robbery. Luscious had heard how "this guy Mario" did it, and everyone at the store had been too terrified to do anything. Yet, a few days later, when Yank and Luscious are holding up a Wal-Mart, a customer draws a weapon on them. Yank shoots him. In the melee the store manager (Barry Corbin) pulls out a gun. Luscious fires and wounds him. Yank and Luscious get away from the Wal-Mart with the cash, and their long killing rampage has begun.

That night in their motel room, while counting their cash, Yank and Luscious watch the news of their heist. They derive an eerie satisfaction from their newfound notoriety. "We're heroes!" Luscious exclaims. They soon plan their next robbery, a shopping mall.

As each botched robbery degenerates into a gunfight, Yank and Luscious begin to take a sick pleasure in the inevitable killing that occurs at each robbery sight. They are always eagerly turning on TVs and radios, or buying newspapers to hear news of their exploits.

As Yank and Luscious commit innumerable grisly murders, the fact that TV cameras follow the killers all over the country (without helping the police stop them) is supposed to be proof positive that Steiger's intended target is the media.

Yet if the "message" of *Serial Murderers Naturally* is that the media is fascinated with violence, the movie offers no moral judgment of the murderers. Insofar as the murderers seem spurred on by the publicity of their crimes, Steiger seems to be suggesting that the media is guiltier than the perpetrators themselves (for giving them the attention they crave).

Yet how does one *not* root for these cold-blooded killers? In the tradition of Warren Beatty and Faye Dunaway in *Bonnie and Clyde* or Paul Newman and Robert Redford in *Butch Cassidy and the Sundance Kid*, Steiger has cast established, likeable stars in the lead roles, urging us to root for the villain-heroes.

With *Serial Murderers Naturally* Steiger created a traditional bloody crime saga, but used the media as his whipping boy so that he wouldn't be accused of utilizing gratuitous violence to draw in audiences. Yet that is precisely what he did, reaping fantastic box-office rewards for his efforts.

Ford

Gerald Ford – Brian Dennehy
Richard Nixon – Anthony Hopkins
Dick Cheney – Dick Cheney
Chevy Chase – Chevy Chase
Written and directed by Jake Steiger

———

Revitalized by the commercial success of *Serial Murders Naturally*, Steiger was artistically confident enough to create *Ford*, a biography of Gerald Ford, the 38th President of the United States.

Brian Dennehy turns in a riveting performance as "Gerry," the former college football star turned politician, who leads America through the turbulent aftermath of Watergate and the OPEC oil crisis.

Early scenes show a troubled Gerry, deliberating with top advisors, such as Chief of Staff Dick Cheney, about whether he should pardon former President Nixon. Ford's unpopular pardon of Nixon is here attributed to heavy pressure from Nixon loyalists in the Administration, who threaten Ford with their collective resignations if Ford fails to save Nixon from jail time.

Despite Steiger drawing some heavy-handed comparisons between Ford and Shakespeare's *King Lear*, Dennehy's powerful performance dramatizes a revisionist view that the bumbling Ford was somehow a masterful politician with a steady hand on the ship of state.

Rather than ignoring it, Steiger wisely depicts Ford's unfortunate tendency to fall down in public. He shows how a few innocent missteps became a national joke due to Chevy Chase's send-up of Ford during the first season of NBC TV's "Saturday Night Live" in 1975-76. An improbable scene shows Chase (played by an aging Chevy Chase) meeting with a high-ranking staffer of the Jimmy Carter campaign—suggesting that a Carter-Chase conspiracy was an "October Surprise" that turned the tide in the 1976 Presidential election, leading to Carter's weak if morally righteous presidency.

Steiger and Dennehy create a Gerald Ford of haunting complexity, breathtaking intellect, and enduring compassion. Curiously, most audiences stayed away.

The Lusitania

Justin Churchland – Leonardo DiCaprio
Julia Richmond – Winona Ryder
Captain Thorne – Max von Sydow
Written, produced, and directed by Steiger

———

Leonardo DiCaprio stars as Justin Churchland, a rich Boston banker's son, who in 1915 wants to visit England despite the Great War raging in Europe. As the mighty *Lusitania* passenger liner leaves New York Harbor (with ominous violins playing over the soundtrack), Justin bumps into a young woman named Julia (Winona Ryder), whom he somehow mistakes for a prostitute. She is humiliated, and so cries and runs away. He feels guilty and stares into the sea.

The opening scenes show us the opulent level of luxury available on passenger liners. Steiger shows us aristocrats shoving shrimp into their mouths while poorer passengers like Julia gape hungrily from a distance, so he appears to be condemning the ways of the degenerate wealthy. A middle-aged American businessman, holding a young nymphet in one hand and a champagne glass in the other laughs, saying "Sometimes I don't think we deserve all this!" Then the camera focuses on the periscope of a nearby German submarine, implying that justice will soon be served.

Late that night, Justin becomes very drunk on champagne. As he is heading back to his cabin he bumps into Julia again, apologizing profusely for having insulted her earlier. She accepts his apology. Soon they are out on the deck, contemplating the dark sea. Justin tries to kiss her. Resisting his amazing wealth, Julia fends him off, asserting her "honor," despite her poverty and obviously tartish manner of dress. But because Justin and Julia bump into each other so often, and because DiCaprio and Ryder's names appear at the top of the movie's credits, we still harbor a suspicion that they will eventually fall in love.

Another subplot follows *The Lusitania*'s Captain Thorne (Max von Sydow), whom we first see reading the Travel section of the *New York Times*. In a nod to historical accuracy, Thorne reads an ad placed by the German Government, warning neutral American travelers of its plans to sink all ships passing through British waters, especially *The Lusitania*. Captain Thorne also knows that stores of American munitions have been secretly stowed in the bowels of his ship (making it a legitimate target under international law). He should warn the unwitting American passengers about the grave dangers of their voyage. But he doesn't tell anyone, knowing he would be fired for leaking the information.

Despite Steiger's efforts at the screenplay level, *The Lusitania* is not a film that will be remembered for its acting. DiCaprio and Ryder's romantic scenes fail to generate any heat. While in the presence of Ryder, DiCaprio's face registers an expression closer to nausea than passion. Ryder herself bears a visible condescension toward the other actors, especially DiCaprio. In interviews after *The Lusitania*'s release, she repeatedly called DiCaprio "talentless," and said that "all she got" out of her own involvement in the movie was her $10 million paycheck, suggesting her lack of artistic fulfillment in making the blockbuster.

The night of the sinking (a heavy-handed caption, "The Night of the Sinking," telegraphs to the audience what is about to happen) Justin finally convinces Julia that he loves her. He convinces her to join him in his cabin.

Soon afterwards a torpedo hits the ship, after which we are engulfed in nearly 45 minutes of splashing water, flying deck chairs, frightened aristocrats in strange hats, men impulsively kissing women or stealing bottles of liquor, and general pandemonium.

Justin vows to never to leave Julia's side. They hold hands tightly. Immediately, an uncannily accurate surge of water bursts into the cabin. The water rushes right at Julia, pushing her away. Their hands grip as long as possible, but eventually Justin's grip slips. Julia is thrust headlong into the Atlantic. Justin cries a little, but manages to find his way to a lifeboat. We sense that his life without Julia will remain a hollow shell.

Indeed, despite the camera's earlier critique of the decadent wealthy, by the end of *The Lusitania* Steiger seems to be offering us the moral of "seize the day." Justin and Julia's only mistake was to let class-consciousness delay their electric passion.

A final caption informs us that over 128 Americans sank to their deaths off the coast of Ireland (the 1,000 dead from other nations are unacknowledged).

The Lusitania gives most viewers an adrenaline rush from the magnificence of its special effects and soundtrack. The ship's sinking is rendered so vividly that we viewers are almost saddened not to have been onboard for such a festival, however fateful.

The Lusitania has set a new technical standard for cinematic entertainment.

Quentin Tarantino Movies

Quentin Tarantino's *Scent of a Banknote*

Mick Jagger – Christopher Walken
Keith Richards – Willem Dafoe
Ron Wood – Quentin Tarantino
Charlie Watts – Christian Slater
Head of the Styx – Cher
Styx Gang Member – Nicholas Cage
Styx Gang Member – Matt Dillon
Police Chief Jackson – Morgan Freeman
Bank Guard – Steve Buscemi
Bank Teller – Maureen Stapleton

Written by Jake Steiger and Quentin Tarantino

Produced and directed by Jake Steiger

———

Director Jake Steiger returned to form with *Scent of a Banknote*. Co-written by rising filmmaker Quentin Tarantino, *Scent of a Banknote* tells the story of two rival LA gangs that rob the same bank at the same time on the same fateful afternoon.

The first half of the movie cuts between shots of each gang planning its respective heist, and features a lot of patented Tarantino dialogue—a colorful blend of gutter profanities and articulation hitherto unseen in cinematic hoods. A great deal of dramatic irony would have been generated in these early scenes had we not already known from previews that both gangs would end up in the bank at the same time.

Christopher Walken stars as the head of the "Stones." They wear Rolling Stones masks during the heist; Walken is Mick Jagger, leader of the gang. Other "Stones" include Tarantino himself, Christian Slater, and Willem Dafoe (a surprisingly plausible Keith Richards). The rival gang, Styx is comprised of Matt Dillon, Nicholas Cage, and Cher (the Dennis DeYoung character), their fiercest, and natural leader.

The Stones arrive at the bank first. Walken seems to be the complete master of the situation until Cher and the other Styx burst into the bank shouting "Everyone on the floor!" At first Cher doesn't notice that the bank is already being robbed. Walken's astonished expression at the Styx' entrance is itself worth the price of admission.

The two gangs—all guns now pointed at each other rather than at bank employees—endure a strangely hilarious 15-minute Mexican stand-off. Walken and Cher spew out menacing (if somewhat eloquent) profanities at each other. The room is charged with the possibility that the two gangs will annihilate each other. No one important is killed yet, except for the obligatory hapless bank-guard (Steve Buscemi), who is shot while reaching for his gun, honorably trying to save the bank that was paying him the minimum wage.

The police soon surround the area, and Walken and Cher realize they had better come to some arrangement. Walken suggests that each gang keep a member of the other gang as hostage; but in a hilarious moment—vintage Tarantino—it becomes apparent that no one in the room cares at all whether *anyone* else lives or dies—thus negating the whole hostage-principle.

Cher (watching her cogitate is one of the great joys of this movie) stumbles upon the brilliant idea of using members of the gangs as fake hostages—just to fool the police. Even the bank employees and customers nod approvingly at this idea, realizing it will relieve them of that thankless task. Walken and Cher phone the police chief (Morgan Freeman), claim they have hostages, and demand a helicopter to the take them to the airport immediately. Now with guns from two rival gangs pointed at her, the bank teller (Maureen Stapleton) is absurdly reduced to counting out equal stacks of money for each gang. "Or Presidents won't be the only dead people on that cash!" yells Walken.

All is going well for the gangs—the cash has been secured, the police believe their story, the helicopter is preparing to land behind the bank—until they realize that some of them are actually going to have to put away their guns and pretend to be hostages. Cher helpfully suggests that all of Walken's "Stones" can be hostages, which only fuels their suspicions of her. They compromise: two members of each gang will be held hostage for appearance's sake. But the "hostages" look so hardened and evil that the police become suspicious.

In the climactic scene (echoing *Dog Day Afternoon*), the helicopter pilot and co-pilot, both undercover policemen, seize an opportune moment (when some of the crooks are already counting the cash) to shoot everyone on board except Walken and Cher. The police themselves are mortally wounded in the melee. Walken pushes the police away and seizes control of the helicopter. Cher pulls her gun on him, but realizes the idiocy of shooting the pilot of the helicopter in which she herself is a passenger. So they form a sort of compact. Cher even claims she has fallen in love with him on this fateful afternoon, to which Walken, resigned to his fate, cynically replies: "Yeah. Until we land."

Scent of a Banknote was nominated for five Academy Awards, including best director (Steiger), best original screenplay (Steiger and Tarantino), best actor (Walken), best supporting actress (Cher), and best cinematography. Many wondered why Cher was considered a *supporting* actress in a movie whose next most prominent female character—Stapleton's hapless bank-teller—has about three minutes of screen time.

132

Quentin Tarantino's *Harder*

Sonny – Harvey Keitel
Slick – Samuel L. Jackson
Lola – Jamie Lee Curtis
Jonesy – Tim Roth

———

Harder, Quentin Tarantino's long-awaited follow-up to *Jackie Brown* and *Pulp Fiction*, features Harvey Keitel as Sonny Graniano, a hardened lifer-convict, who is accidentally paroled due to a Y2K bug in the California State Prison System's computers.

Sonny's cellmate, "Slick" (Samuel L. Jackson) had once told him about his hidden cache of diamonds in LA, believing Sonny would never be released. As Sonny is escorted to freedom, Slick hangs from his cell bars and threatens him in the awesome cadence of an Old Testament prophet: "If you take my rocks, I will search the sun, the moon, and the stars and cut thee down with a mighty hand!"—to which Sonny smiles condescendingly as he walks away to freedom.

Sonny quickly makes his way to LA, cruising down the freeway, singing along mirthfully to forgotten classic rock songs of the 1970s (all of which appear on the new *Harder* soundtrack). The audience is supposed to be struck by the incongruities in Sonny's character: soulful singer yet a convict, militant anti-smoker yet a raging alcoholic.

Sonny encounters a motley assortment of low-life characters during his quest for the diamonds, including Jonesy, an animated cartoon aficionado/incipient heroin addict (Tim Roth), and the ravishing Lola (Jamie Lee Curtis), the custodian of Slick's diamonds and his former lover. Jonesy breaks into an ostensibly hilarious monologue about the aesthetic superiority of "The Flintstones" over "The Simpsons," and offers further proof of his (and Tarantino's) intimacy with popular culture.

Jamie Lee Curtis' Lola convincingly pretends to be a clueless wench, concealing from Sonny the whereabouts of the diamonds. But her grating, whiny voice drives Sonny to paroxysms of rage. After she smokes in his new Ford Taurus one too many times, Sonny empties his Smith & Wesson revolver into her torso (prompting hysterical laughter, loud applause, and even cheers in the audience). But in an ironic reversal, Sonny takes a Camel Light from Lola's bloody pack, and like a true Tarantino character, smokes with a gusto that presages a sudden addiction.

Meanwhile, Slick has escaped from jail, and assembled a new gang to kill Sonny and to secure the diamonds. Slick exhorts his troops violently, using the "n-word" more times than the word "the."

With Lola dead, Sonny ransacks her apartment, and discovers the key to a locker at a local gun club, where he is sure the diamonds are hidden. Sonny,

133

Slick and his gang, and the police (who are tailing Sonny for Lola's murder) all arrive at the gun club simultaneously. A three-way shoot-out erupts, and the gun club is nearly destroyed, inciting many civilian gun club patrons to fire back out of sheer moral indignation (making it now a four-way gun fight).

After an epic shooting spree that spans nearly 15 minutes of screen time, only Sonny and Slick are still alive, though both have been mortally wounded. The bloody bag of diamonds lies on the floor between them. Slick says the diamonds will go to the "harder man," to which Sonny replies: "I'm harder. I'm *Sonny*, hard as the rocks that squeezed them diamonds hard"—an insane utterance that visibly perplexes the wounded Slick.

Then—each predator apparently satisfied that he has frightened the other with ominous words—they fire off their last rounds of ammunition, missing completely. They both crawl along the floor, smearing blood everywhere. Slick opens the bag, only to find glass cubes and a note that says: "Sorry Slick—Love, Lola." Sonny and Slick eye each other, momentarily united by a mutual hatred of the dead Lola, before they both die.

Tim Roth's addled heroin addict/cartoon critic then emerges from the shadows, opens another locker containing the real diamonds, walks calmly to his Isuzu Rodeo, and drives into the sunset to the tune of Pink Floyd's "Shine On You Crazy Diamond—Part 3."

Harder shows that Tarantino can still deliver all that is expected of him: ignorance-validating references to popular culture, a lucrative use of product placement, neo-post-ironic asides in lieu of emotional engagement, and violence so gratuitous that now well-trained Tarantino audiences laugh like seals at his inhuman audacity.

Harder is another sure-fire Tarantino blockbuster.

Reviews of Imaginary Books

Review: John Irving's *The Third Leg*

John Irving's latest book, *The Third Leg*, depicts the life of John Bath, an aging, award-winning writer, struggling with his literary destiny and his unusual family. As the novel opens, Bath is grappling with his next opus, *The Vienna Circus Rape*, but is distracted by critics' accusations that his sensationalist plots pander to popular taste.

John Bath is the head of another eccentric Irving family. At 28, his son, Martin, is already a famous writer, but has been labeled pejoratively as "a minor, Canadian Stephen King." His second wife, Anneke, is a Dutch doctor, a prosthetist, whom Bath met in Amsterdam while on a book tour. His daughter, Hannah, is inexplicably single and celibate, despite being 32, a surgeon, and stunningly attractive.

Martin Bath is homosexual, and for all John's oft-spoken tolerance, he is secretly uncomfortable that his only biological son is gay. John thinks himself manly, and after Martin's coming out party he indulges in a bit of extramarital philandering, almost as if to reassure himself of his own heterosexuality. John shares with Martin an interest in both writing and body piercing, but they fail to connect emotionally.

Martin's partner, a mercurial Austrian named Hans, has been walking on a prosthetic leg since the age of 15. In early chapters, Hans catches his peg leg in a broken sidewalk grate, as well as a golf hole, leading to characteristic Irving slapstick and mayhem. Anneke offers to equip Hans with a new leg, one with which he can swap out the tip for various accessories, including a pool cue.

John's daughter, Hannah, then re-enters the novel, bringing home an Indian mystery writer, Ketan, who shares some uncanny similarities with Salman Rushdie, such as having had death threats issued against him because of his writing. It is well known in the family that Hannah and Ketan have never consummated their relationship. Ketan, an upholder of traditional Indian values, is still trying to convince his indifferent parents to orchestrate an arranged marriage with Hannah.

Then Toronto is rocked by a murder mystery: a young homosexual man is discovered in a meat locker. He had been gored by a deep spear-like weapon. To their horror, Anneke and the Baths begin to suspect that Hans committed the murder with his old prosthetic leg, the one Anneke herself had recently replaced, effectively disposing of the evidence. Ketan spearheads an independent investigation into the murder, mainly in the hopes of clearing Hans, who is now held by the police.

The murder mystery is suddenly interrupted as the story returns to the subplot of John Bath's writer's block. He is still obsessed with his first book, *Breakfast at the Schumann's*, which he feels he has never equaled. In that work he had already tied together his lifelong themes, and never again so tightly and purely. Each work after *Schumann* appeared as a kind of pastiche of disjointed themes: dead parents, broken families, and literally broken people—dismemberment featuring in nearly all of his novels alongside the semi-obligatory rape or two.

John's creative sterility is further underscored after Martin suddenly produces a small literary novel, *Broken Twigs in the Grass*, to near universal acclaim. The literary critics now compare Martin favorably to John, even if John's sensationalist soap operas disguised as novels are best-sellers.

So John can no longer work on his sunset opus, *The Vienna Circus Rape*, set in fin de siècle Vienna and featuring a pre-*Interpretation of Dreams* Sigmund Freud. Bath is stuck on the key scene where Sigmund and his wife, Martha, have a domestic spat. Martha attacks Sigmund with a menorah, nearly poking out both his eyes—an incident which purportedly has a seminal impact on Freud's theories.

As usual, Irving's denouement is worthy of Dickens. Although I won't spoil the ending, Hans' peg leg proves to be a Cinderella-like fit that ties up all loose plot threads.

The Third Leg published two years after *The Fourth Hand*, continues Irving's theme of dismemberment. But the Bath family reveals little inspiration. Some readers may squirm at scenes that seem like straight autobiography.

It's impossible not to like Irving's characters. They are smart, well-spoken, affluent, good-looking, and fully developed. Their lives are filled with interesting problems that the characters have the time and resources to solve.

However, as Irving revisits the same themes again, the seams of his craftsmanship are more apparent, perhaps distracting some readers. *The Third Leg* is Irving's weakest work to date. We hope that Irving can dig deep into himself to discover new themes after a lifetime of writing and reflection.

Lost William Faulkner Novel Found?

JACKSON, MISSISSIPPI—An academic conference, "Incest, Murder and Mutes in Faulkner's Early Fiction" was held here last week to discuss an astonishing development in the history of Faulkner scholarship—the possible discovery of a previously unknown Faulkner manuscript entitled *Sons of the South*. The novel, written during the years 1926-1928, will be published this month by the University of Mississippi Press. It is still not entirely clear whether or not the author was really Faulkner or some imitator.

Sons of the South tells the story of four generations of a great southern family, the McAlisters, as seen through the eyes of Uncle Slokum McAlister, one of the last of the line. As the novel begins, Uncle Slokum is dying, and babbling in a fit of delirium. Discovering him on death's door is young Billy McAlister, an illiterate mute and distant relative, who nurses him into a state of semi-lucidity. Fortified by whiskey, Uncle Slokum begins telling his great-nephew the history of their family in Mississippi.

The McAlister dynasty begins when Colonel Robert Louis McAlister and his family arrive in Mississippi from South Carolina. We learn that McAlister ("Sweet Bobby Lou" to his lovers) is an insatiable philanderer and expert marksman, and this combination of traits provides him many chances to engage in dueling. Soon after arriving in Mississippi, McAlister dispatches an aging and heirless landowner with one shot, and assumes his estate. Colonel McAlister proves to be an unstoppable life-force who not only develops a mighty plantation, but also finds time to sleep with his wife, mistresses, and slaves, spawning a vast brood of children (ten sons and three daughters from eight different women—none of them his wife) within a fifteen year span.

Uncle Slokum is an expansive narrator, prone to digression, and willing to confess the most appalling incidents from his own life. We soon learn that Slokum himself is an eccentric and cad of regional reputation, whose own sexual predations rival even those of the great family patriarch, his grandfather, Colonel McAlister. There are strong suggestions of incest and hints at bestiality. Slokum, in his drunken delirium, even mistakes the unwashed Billy for a father confessor, there to absolve him or administer last rites. But Slokum's own narrative drive keeps him going.

We finally learn that old Colonel McAlister makes his fatal mistake when he impregnates the wife of a wealthy banker, who ends McAlister's life and dueling career with two quick shots. The death of Colonel McAlister causes a dynastic crisis, as he left behind ten young illegitimate sons, but no legitimate heirs. Seven of the ten sons were named Bobby Lou by their adoring mothers.

His wife Sarah's quiet response to his serial philandering is to outlive Colonel McAlister by 44 years, during which time she sees this baroque family tree explode beyond the mental faculties of anyone (including the narrator,

Uncle Slokum, and perhaps even the author) to keep track of. Editors have founds several drafts of family tree diagrams in his notes, but disagree on which one is final, and so none will be included in the novel's first edition.

Uncle Slokum's narrative ultimately reaches a point of hopeless confusion. With ultimately four generations of fathers and sons named Bobby Lou, Slokum's erratic digressions through nearly 100 years of family history sometimes makes it impossible to determine even in which century certain incidents take place.

What is clear is that Colonel McAlister's eldest, white, illegitimate son, Bobby Lou, assumes the helm of the family in this characteristic sentence fragment:

> ...and he, Bobby Lou, bayou born and bred, legitimate not by law but by default and lack of law; barely fifteen and a blushing boy virgin to whom the McAlisters' rivals in Yoknapawtapha County paid neither heed nor mind nor tribute nor respect, clopped his new store-bought boots on the front porch of the plantation house to address the assembled congregation, his family and servants, many of them his half-brothers and sisters, likewise sons and daughters of freshly-dead Colonel Robert Louis McAlister—yet he, young Bobby Lou, the butt of boyhood games, a mere hook-baiter for his slave cousins Old Joseph, Corn Bread, and Hammer Joe, his seniors as men and fishermen, with a pipe too large for his beardless face, now their titular lord and master, in his first act of manhood, spoke to them in the sunshine of the May dawn... (*Sons of the South*, 445)

Bobby Lou the Eldest proves an able administrator, and the family's wealth grows under his leadership. However, the Civil War breaks out and "Bobby Lou II" is killed at the siege of Fort Henry in 1862. Bobby Lou II leaves behind no male heirs, and so Juan Roberto Salvador ("Chico") McAlister, Colonel McAlister's second eldest illegitimate son through a Mexican prostitute, asserts his rights to the McAlister empire. Chico oversees the freeing of the slaves in 1865, but is soon deposed by the alliance of a freed slave woman JoJo (who seduces Chico), and Rufus McAlister, a distant cousin (who pole-axes him).

Rufus, a raging alcoholic even by McAlister standards, presides over the long, steady decline in the family fortunes, and his low wattage vitality yields only one son, Slokum, who is widely suspected of being adopted or a foundling.

Even without narrating his own early life, Slokum emerges as one of the most challenging narrators in 20th century literature. His nearly eight-hundred pages of McAlister family history clearly stands as a direct challenge to Joyce's *Ulysses* as the most challenging read of the 1920s, if not the century. Slokum describes several key events, such as Colonel McAlister's fatal duel, or his own whiskey-induced conversion to Catholicism, many times, and each telling varies in critical details.

Things are further confused by the author's occasional intrusion in the narration (such as in the fragment above), which resembles Slokum's style closely enough that we are sometimes not sure whether the author or Slokum is addressing us.

Finally, a now-senile Uncle Slokum comes to believe that he himself is the long-dead Colonel McAlister. He relates events *in the first person* ("When I fought against the Yankees...") of which he has only third-hand knowledge from his grandfather.

Sons of the South suggests profound insights about the role of the narrator in literary fiction. By having Slokum relate the entire McAlister history to dumb and illiterate Billy, Faulkner elegantly comments on the one-sided nature of the writer-reader relationship: every reader is an end-in-himself— unable to propagate the tale being told, or even comprehend it.

How, we may wonder, does this text exist if Slokum tells it only to an illiterate mute just before he dies?

Only time will tell whether *Sons of the South* is studied with the same devotion as Faulkner's avowed masterworks, but this new discovery may shed light on the development of one of America's greatest novelists.

Review: Thomas Pynchon's *Dys*

A new Thomas Pynchon work is always an event, and his devoted readers will treasure his latest effort, *Dys*. *Dys* is clearly dystopian fiction, but it is still a Pynchon work more than anything else—a wickedly funny masterpiece about power, history, and conspiracy. The picture of encroaching fascism in America that Pynchon sketched in his underappreciated *Vineland* has been painted more luridly in *Dys*.

Americans in *Dys* live in constant fear and shock, in a state of perpetual war, and under the eyes of increasingly penetrating electronic surveillance. The skies are policed by millions of pesky VDs (flying video drones), which spot-check everyone's behavior on a daily basis. But Americans have taken the surveillance in stride; the home version of VDs (packaged as flying pigs) are hot sellers in the burgeoning personal reconnaissance market. Everyone is spying on each other. Life is like the movie *The Truman Show*, except that *everyone* is on TV (or the web).

In *Dys*, everyone except the super-rich live under VD surveillance, the images from which can be seen instantly over the internet to anyone who tunes into a person's VD cam site. Everyone watches everyone else (and himself) on TV. If *Vineland* described the mind-deadening banality of TV, TV in *Dys* is mostly surveillance footage, war footage, or *COPS Around the Clock*™.

Like many Pynchon works, the story is a quest, this time of a young woman (Ginger Vitis) looking for her husband (Ellsworth Vitis), a leftist writer. Ellsworth is captured from their Florida home by paramilitary forces in a pre-dawn raid. Ginger works her way through labyrinthine bureaucracies encountering only stony silences about Ellsworth's capture. The Federal Police finally produce some "evidence" concerning his disappearance, but Ginger identifies these as crude forgeries, especially Ellsworth's ridiculous "prophecy" that he will be captured by Pakistani militants *posing* as paramilitary police, or his obviously doctored "suicide note."

Frustrated by attempts to discover her husband's whereabouts, Ginger begins researching Constitutional law in order to determine her legal strategy to get Ellsworth back. She soon learns that the Patriot Act has dissolved the Bill of Rights. ("Wow! *That* wasn't on TV," she laments.) She begins to devour works about the 1960s, a time before her birth that she believes represented the American people's final attempt to resist state power. Watching the video drones hover outside her window, she is comforted by the thought that a free society was once possible.

With her life destroyed, Ginger accepts the offer of her college roommate, Dizzy Trollope, now a graduate student in history, to visit her in Amsterdam. In Amsterdam, Ginger and Dizzy are free to talk, even if their passports have embedded GPS technology to track their whereabouts, and most of the city center is under VD surveillance. In Dizzy's apartment, they smoke semi-legal Dutch marijuana, while Dizzy, who has been researching "The Plot" for years, tells her friend the "true history of the world."

Dizzy has seen the archives of a secret society now known only as The Plot. The Plot experienced many name changes, but was started in 18th century France by a group of seminary students devoted to interpreting Nostradamus' *Centuries*. The exegetes violently debated the meaning of some quatrains. Extremists vowed to actively fulfill the apocalyptic prophecies. A secret committee created a blueprint for world domination, which they estimated would take about 250 years to execute.

The seminarians' plan to infiltrate secret societies, international banking and diplomatic circles, the press, The Church, and global intelligence operations.

Dizzy's long monologue traces The Plot from the French and American Revolutions through the present day. Even "the Holy Sixties themselves," Dizzy says, were just another state media production of The Plot (however real the revolutionary vibes seemed at the time). The countercultural leaders of the 1960's were usually CIA operatives. Gloria Steinem? CIA. Bummer.

Ginger is skeptical about most of these theories. She is further confused by listening to other weird theories from Dizzy's wacky Dutch friends, Jaap and Saskia. Saskia believes The Plot didn't start with the French at all, but with a mysterious group known only as the GDG based in 17th century Amsterdam.

While conspiracy buffs may drink in these tantalizing suggestions like mother's milk, others are left uncertain as to Pynchon's intentions. While we share his concerns about civil liberties, how much of Dizzy's pot-addled conspiracy does Pynchon (expect us to) take seriously? Is he encouraging us to research history, or is he only trumpeting his theme of history as fiction?

We're not sure, but at least Pynchon allows his characters and readers a spark of hope. The deeper Ginger and Dizzy probe into the conspiracy, the more they encounter the forces of entropy undermining the totalitarian leviathan. Even among the Elite, the 100 families that Dizzy believes run the world, there remains a refreshingly human tendency for intrigue and internecine warfare.

For a determined truth-seeker such as Ginger, the system actually proves porous enough that she finally discovers Ellsworth, still alive, but now exposed for having sinister connections to German pharmaceutical companies.

Pynchon maintains his high standards for density, allusion, and humor. Pynchon here is as multi-dimensional as ever. He can describe dark settings and actions, and also display his more ludic side. But some readers may find his habits irritating. He relishes spoofing TV shows and inventing ridiculous song lyrics. He gives his characters flat, silly names that weaken their emotive impact.

Despite these criticisms, Pynchon is clearly one of the few living masters. *Dys* is a dense textual tapestry. Urgency informs this work, as if Pynchon is aware that his efforts to warn us about encroaching state power are far too late. *Dys* gives us a strong suggestion of how Pynchon views our new Orwellian realities, such as the Patriot Act, the Department of Stateside Security, and the War on Terrorism.

Poems

Saint Nicholas and Count Monet

(As told by Saint Nicholas)

Saint Nicholas brings gifts to both humble and great
and poems that reveal their bad character traits.
He tries the hot air from their egos to deflate,
to change their behavior before it's too late;
to show them there's a path both righteous and straight,
for as Philosophers say: "Character is Fate."

Count Monet was a banker of astonishing greed.
He cared not a whit for poor people in need.
He offered them loans with print too small to read,
the interest compounding at mind-boggling speed!

He squeezed the poor so hard that he thought they'd bleed.
Yet for breakfast on champagne and oysters he'd feed.
And he said to himself: "I'm the best of my breed!"

Since all the poor people in his debts did drown,
he served as *de facto* ruler of town.
So I gave to Count Monet a King's golden crown.
He wore the crown in his Lear jet while he flew all around.
He ignored the people walking round with a frown,
and he refused the debts of the town to write down.

Since I knew his soul suffered from rot and gangrene,
and I wanted his small, greedy heart to come clean,
I brought him a statue of a well-balanced Queen,
Queen Justice herself, all blind and serene:
To show him higher powers would soon intervene
if his Ponzi Schemes grew ever more Byzantine.

Monet placed "Queen Justice" in his Corporate cantine;
then gave a speech about "Justice" while wired on caffeine
called "Money is Justice: What Else Could it Mean?"
And though he had wealth so immense and obscene,
while the people of the town looked hungry and lean,
he still wouldn't stop his hot money machine.

So the next year I gave him a gold Bishop's mitre,
a hat just like mine, but mine's ten kilos lighter.
I hoped he'd become a great spiritual fighter
against poverty, and make the town's future brighter.
But he sold my gold hat to a loan underwriter.
And the door to his heart and his checkbook closed tighter.

Count Monet showed little signs of remorse.
He was on the wrong track, but wouldn't change course!
He clearly still loved The Dark Side of The Force.
So the next year I brought him a huge Trojan Horse.
I filled it with money that he had won on the Bourse.
It looked like a large chess knight, carved crudely and coarse.

But Monet was unmoved by all that Baksheesh.
He shipped that Trojan Horse back to Old Greece,
to push loans at high interest, so more people he'd fleece,
trading great stacks of paper for their last silver piece.
And no matter how high the Misery Index increased
He refused to make the whole debt cycle cease.

Still Monet was not happy, don't ask me why,
after those profits he skimmed from the money supply.
He'd built a new Castle, a bit bigger than Versailles.
But when his tax bill came he'd whine and he'd cry:
"No one has done more for the people than I!
I *won't* pay these taxes. I'd just rather die!"

So I brought a sand Castle on a large silver tray
to show him one day it would all melt away;
that despite his incredible wealth on display,
his castle was a prison to keep people at bay.
And now he was growing alone and so gray,
that time marched on and he *would* die one day.
And all this Bad Karma he'd still have to repay—
in a manner of speaking, not by reincarnation *per se*.

His response to these warnings was a rude, gaping yawn.
So I brought a bronze statue in the shape of a Pawn,
carved with Monet's own face: sad, old and withdrawn.
I left it right there on his great castle lawn,
hoping new feelings in his heart to spawn.
And the light of his conscience *did* finally dawn!

"Saint Nicholas! I see I'm a total disgrace!
I can see it written right on my unhappy face.
I've slaved away my life in this stupid rat-race!
But never again shall I the world's credit debase!
I must give my fellow man a kindly embrace,
before I say my final good-bye to this place.

"This Pawn taught me that I too have been used.
The Castle showed my values have been totally confused.
The Horse: that strange gifts might best be refused;
The Bishop's Hat: that my spirit should be far more enthused;
Queen Justice: that my crimes will not be lightly excused;
The King's crown: that my ego was so gross that it oozed."

Monet feared the End Game on a board full of regrets.
So he gave away all of his castles and his jets.
He gave me back the gold hats and Chess statuettes,
and stopped treating the people like his personal pets.
He agreed to cancel everyone's outstanding debts.
For Saint Nicholas Justice: that's as good as it gets.

Thirteen Ways of Looking at a Tax Return

(With apologies to Wallace Stevens' "Thirteen Ways of Looking at a Blackbird")

I.
April is the cruelest month,
when youthful hearts with passion burn,
and everyone else must
file an income tax return.

II.
Draft versions of her tax return,
lie crumpled on the table,
stained by her coffee cup,
like pages from an unfinished fiction.

III.
A man and a woman
are one.
A man and a woman and a tax return
are one (if filing jointly).

IV.
She thought secrets
more guarded than diaries
are locked away in our hearts,
and found in our tax returns.

V.
She remembered the old Zen koan:
"What is the sound of one hand clapping?"
And thought of her own:
"What is the sound of a tax return,
in a strong wind, flapping?"

VI.
Over dinner, beside the vase full of tulips,
the lilac-smelling candles slowly burn,
casting massive flower-shaped shadows
upon their white tax return.

VII.
That night she dreamt:
a vivid nightmare about an audit,
a tax inspector saw her tax return,
flying around like a paper airplane,
and he caught it.

VIII.
The tax inspector began with a wicked grin:
"Our data shows that the act of filing
stops most people from smiling."

IX.
"You look sad, but have no regrets!
The tax you pay will service
the interest on our national Debt,
for at least a few seconds, I'll bet!"

X.
He took out a magnifying glass and cackled with joy:
"The Income tax is the most awesome tool
that the State can employ:
'The power to tax is the power to destroy.'"[14]

XI.
"And what have we here?
I think you've been cheating.
You can't deduct all those steaks
you've been eating!"

XII.
In the morning she awoke with profound relief.
No tax inspectors were calling her a thief.
She rushed to her table to review her tax forms,
She checked that she followed all GAAP norms.

XIII.
And finally, with a shaking hand,
she signed the thing
she could not understand.

---

[14] *McCulloch v. Maryland*, 17 U.S. 316 (1819).

Lost in Florida

Fast Food Satori

I pulled into a McDonald's near Disney World and walked into the white-lit restaurant, nearly slipping on the wet soapy tile. I got in line and saw from the Ronald McDonald clock (pointing with gangling, white-gloved arms) that it was 4:10. The beginnings of a pre-dinner rush were queued up before the registers. I stood in line behind a crown-bald, spectacled businessman, who ordered a chef salad with two dressings. My air-conditioned nightmare began.

I finally got to order, and a pretty young girl with a tight, striped uniform told me it'd just take a minute. So I took a dutiful step to the side while she scurried around behind the counter gathering Styrofoam cups and chocolate shakes. I looked over the steel rampart food storage bins to see the cooks and other untouchables. Most of them wore a cynically-glum grin, as if all the orders coming in were some colossal joke that they had little to do with. Occasionally I'd see some upstart, busily efficient, working around his associates to snappily wrap a special burger, and announce its birth with a well-drilled, monotone corporate voice.

I rested my hands on the sponge-streaked, stainless-steel counter, noting that the assistant manager was wearing a headset to help handle the drive-thru orders. She looked like the radio operator in an infantry unit. I thought myself to be a model of patience, watching trucker dudes who had been behind me in the line take away their sacked goodies and smirk at me with a faint air of We Got Fast Food condescension. Though travelling and in a hurry myself, I just turned and smiled at the napkin dispenser, taking a few too many napkins—more to pass the time than out of need. My little cashier friend no longer seemed to know me or even see me, and I looked at Ronald on the clock to see that it was 4:17. I took in the crew at a glance: face-down burger flippers gloriously indifferent, stiff slacked cashiers turning robotically to fill drinks with a single button-touch, and the captain, immersed in orders that seemed pressing enough to be coming from Mrs. Kroc's mansion.

I watched the last of the batch of French fries get scooped away to reveal a salty sediment on the steel bin. I felt a pang of impatience now, but sighed anthropologically—damn well ready to wait and see how long I would be set out to dry before the tiny female hand would proffer my hot bag of joy.

A crowd of people now flowed in, and with seemingly supersensory antennae, the crew kitchen pullulated, as if they were a team of stopgaps plugging the dike for the onrushing flood. I now felt hopeless, and began to stare at my cashier, as if—fool—that would get her attention.

She missed me completely, stopped, and said "Can I take your order?" implying to her current customer that it would be great if he could hurry the hell up about it. After she took his money, she turned so quickly that I couldn't indulge my impulse to touch her doll's arm and give her a pathetic, pleading expression.

Watching the buzz of the mob in line and the blur of blue-legged workers behind the counter, I suddenly felt absolutely detached from the scene—so apart that I was sure I wasn't even there, as if I were having an out-of-body experience. I looked into the eyes of people behind the counter, almost hoping someone would notice me. For a second I lost my balance and had to catch myself from falling.

Futile. Had I *died* or something? Was I experiencing a Buddhist enlightenment? Now? In McDonald's? Although largely ignorant about Buddhism, I thought it was possible. I felt the blood rush to my head. It would befit the Universal Irony if my Enlightenment came while waiting in line at a McDonald's.

For all its frenzy, the white-lit scene froze into a tableau. My chest caged hot breath. I turned and looked and saw Ronald's arms pointing at numbers on the clock. 4:20. Time. How reassuring.

Then I shouted, in a cracked voice, to no one in particular: "Hey! I've been waiting here for ten minutes!"

Everyone in line looked at me, some as if they were afraid of me. My cashier turned from pouring coffee, her face working, trying to remember me.

"Oh. I'm sorry. What did you order?"

"Quarter pounder with cheese, large fries, large coke."

As she gathered my food products, reality snapped into place. I turned to look at the impatient people behind me. Their own palpable sense of hurry affirmed our common humanity.

The cashier handed me my purchase brusquely enough to crush my secret hope for a free chocolate shake for my trouble.

My First Cubicle

Golden Publishing recruited the foolhardy and the destitute, the bungled and the botched, and then held their employees in a tight vise of hopelessness. Desperate job-seekers were attracted by its "Help Wanted" box in the Sunday paper:

Help Wanted

- 6 Editors
- 6 Copy Editors
- 6 Proofreaders

Contact: Golden Publishing

The ad created the impression of an expanding business, one with so many open positions that you just might have a chance at *one* at them. The reality was that the turnover was so high that it was impossible to keep all the positions filled. The exact same ad ran for 75 consecutive Sundays during my year-and-a-half stint there. Seeing the three "6s" in a row (666) in the ad, I tried to forget my fundamentalist Christian upbringing and not feel any ill omens.

Golden Publishing was a place of the damned, the down-sized, the newly-divorced, or in my case, simply the naïve. I was 25 when I worked there. Employees found it hard to respect each other, to overcome the vapid expressions that revealed the obvious lack of self-esteem or marketable skills that kept us there.

Thousands of people were moving to Central Florida every week, and most of the available jobs were at Disney World, or in food service, maid service, or telemarketing. Florida called itself a "Right to Work State"—an Orwellian euphemism that I was told meant that high wages and unionization were discouraged.

I had already worked an odd assortment of jobs in Florida during my first six months there: telemarketer (1.5 days), medical transcriptionist (3 weeks), T-shirt attendant at the Harley-Davidson Southern HOG Rally (1 week), photo-copier (6 hours), phone-dialer at the Sprint Booth at the Daytona 500 (3 days), and others too humiliating to recount.

Nonetheless, my first cubicle was at Golden Publishing, as an "editor" of statute books. The Goldens published criminal and motor vehicle law books that policemen apparently tossed into the backseat of patrol cars and referred to from time to time.

I admit that for my first day or two I was impressed that I was an "editor," but it quickly became clear that this was a glorified title. I was really a copy editor, and the "writers" I edited were state legislatures. Actually, I just had to reproduce whatever the legislatures produced, no matter how botched the grammar, reasoning or the injustice of the new laws. On big days, I got to make an editorial note about the law's effective date.

On my first day Mr. Golden handed me two things: a razor-blade and a rival publisher's *Compiled Statutes of Connecticut for Lawyers*. My mission was to slice out the pages of the Connecticut state code comprising the Criminal and Motor Vehicle titles, place them one-by-one on a flat-bed scanner, and scan them in. My two weeks' labor at the scanner would become the electronic foundation of the Goldens' own *Connecticut Criminal and Motor Vehicle Laws for Non-Lawyers*—after I had cleaned up two bazillion errors created by the crude scanning technology of the time.

After I cleaned up all the errors, Mr. Golden himself would personally add a few "deliberate errors," he called them, which supposedly would help him catch any renegade publisher who had attempted to copy from the Goldens' crudely doctored volume.

Even *imagining* the sort of publisher that would steal from the Goldens' books proved beyond my powers. After personally preparing some of the abortions that the Goldens marketed and sold, my trusty razor-blade and I had first-hand knowledge of their low quality.

How could an underpaid, unappreciated workforce produce professional work? (Actually, because we were paid so low, we were granted seemingly endless time to finish each project, and so some of the editors were conscientious to the point of neurosis—their pride in their work being their last bastion of self-esteem.)

In addition to the low pay, there was also the gallingly bleak benefits package. This was posted in a document near the time-clock, alongside the company's policies. This made sense since so many of the benefits were conditional on punching in and out properly anyway.

The Golden Publishing benefits package consisted of:

* No sick days;
* No vacation;
* No retirement benefits of any kind;
* No life insurance;
* No vision or dental benefits
* Health Insurance, in the form of a stingy HMO;
* Six paid Holidays: New Year's Day, Memorial Day, Independence Day, Labor Day, Thanksgiving, and Christmas. Holiday pay was contingent on your working full weeks before and after any holiday. Many people failed to work full weeks around these holidays and thus received no holiday pay.

Other featured company policies included:

- Mandatory punching in and out each day, including for lunch;
- No scheduled breaks (two five-minute smoking breaks permitted);
- No possibility of advancement;
- No hope.

I tried to read the entire list of rules one day, but Mr. Golden walked by, and asked me to go back to work in his reluctantly tyrannical way.

Golden Publishing was a family business, run by Mrs. and Mr. Golden and their son, Brice. It was clear to me right away that Mrs. Golden wore the pants in the family. Mrs. Golden hired me.

"We'll try it," she shrugged, after looking into my desperate haven't-worked-in-months eyes.

It was true; I hadn't worked in months. I had even driven 40 miles to my interview, my old Cadillac leaking gasoline the whole way. I would have to yank the steering wheel suddenly to avoid the toss of a lit cigarette butt from the driver of the pickup truck speeding in front of me, displaying his Confederate flag bumper stickers on the gun rack. I vividly imagined the lit cigarette butt bouncing under my car and achieving a direct hit on the hole on my gas tank and causing a massive explosion. I was often dodging such thoughtfully tossed cigarettes. Nonetheless, I myself smoked in the incredible leaking Cadillac.

The fact that I now drove 40 miles each way in order to be exploited was a truly humiliating daily proposition.

So as I walked out to my car at the end of a workday, I was almost glad to see the pool of gasoline under my car. It was if my Cadillac had taken a leak on the Goldens' property. "Good Cadillac," I'd encourage it as I entered the unlocked car. Of course, I could only drive one mile away from the Golden compound before I'd have to stop at the gas station and fill up the twenty gallon tank for the next few days. Unfortunately, I wasn't paid enough to get my car fixed for a while, so I leaked a fair portion of my wages onto the Florida highways.

#

Mrs. Golden wore business suits and walked on stout legs and heels with a regally slow bearing. She had a round face on a round head of graying hair, thick as a babushka, cut down to the globe-size mop she wore. Her eyes remained stern, focused and alert during almost all interaction with her employees—even while exchanging greetings—as if any perceived sign of weakness would result in more people asking for raises. Occasionally, such as the times I talked to her about the art reproductions on her wall, her eyes sparkled with gaiety despite herself—or perhaps it was just the light reflecting off her glasses, I can't be sure.

Mrs. Golden walked around every Friday morning to pass out our checks to us. She would smile grimly as she handed us the clipboard, on which she insisted we sign a statement that we had both received our paychecks, and that we acknowledged that we had not been harassed in any manner the prior week—which some employees felt itself was a form of harassment.

She would say a few things to us—mixing with the commoners, as it were. It was clear this pained her. I learned that she came from old money, and owned millions of dollars' worth of real estate. Golden Publishing seemed like a front or base for their far wider field of operations, whatever those were. These other ventures were probably what the Goldens screamed at each other about all the time.

Once I overheard Mrs. Golden scream: "Sam! I *told you* we should have sued those bastards!"—as if this were their standard procedure from which they had foolishly deviated due to Sam's cowardice.

I never heard Mr. Golden (Sam) talk back to his wife. He was the more passive creature, roaming the labyrinthine halls of the Golden compound in his sneakers, invariably wearing brown dress pants of cheap hybrid-materials, and white dress shirts sporting unfashionably long collars. His black hair obstinately refused to comply with his half-hearted comb-over. Usually a layer of wispy strands of hair would stick up into the air. It might even flop around while he talked to you, requiring discipline to not laugh or to not follow the flopping hair with your eyes. The skin around his eyes was permanently crinkled but there was plaintiveness in his eyes. While looking at him I was invariably reminded of Yoda from the *Star Wars* movies, though he didn't have Yoda's aspect of wisdom.

Mr. Golden was more apt to walk around quacking "What?! What?!" like a wayward penguin. He might not speak with you for weeks, but then might take a sudden interest in the book you were editing. Then he would offer a rapid series of inappropriate suggestions for expediting the book's completion, suggestions you could only hope he would promptly forget—and then he would forget, and might not speak with you again for several weeks. Like Mrs. Golden, perhaps his mentor in these matters, Mr. Golden conveyed the impression he didn't know who you were—any sort of relationship might make a slight prick in his conscience, and force him to give you more money.

The Goldens were nothing if not cost-conscious. On one occasion, the production staff was rushing out copies of the *Illinois Criminal and Motor Vehicle Code for Dummies* in order to meet a strict deadline. There was no problem except for the gloss covers, which took many hours to dry on their own. The production staff usually sprayed an aerosol sealant on the book covers to accelerate their drying time, but after they ran out of the aerosol, Mr. Golden became desperate.

Not wanting to spend the time or money to acquire more of the fast-working aerosol, Mr. Golden brought a few copies of the book into the kitchen. A few production staff watched in awe as Mr. Golden placed a copy of the *Illinois Criminal and Motor Vehicle Code for Dummies* into the microwave, selected a heating time, and pressed the Start button. After a few moments,

Mr. Golden removed the melting experiment from the appliance, threw the book in the trash, and ran cursing out of the kitchen. One of the pressmen, aware of the workers' interest in collecting Golden artifacts, retrieved the book as evidence of their inventiveness. But what if the experiment had worked? The mind reels at the thought of the makeshift assembly line Mr. Golden might have fashioned in order to microwave 2,500 copies of the *Illinois Criminal and Motor Vehicle Code for Dummies.*

Perhaps it would be the same kind of workflow he used to salvage the occasional unused stamp from the daily mail. After the three Goldens had finished opening their daily load of mail, and had personally fed any envelopes from compromising sources into their paper shredders, two people from the production staff were called to pick up the opened envelopes. Then they were to stand and scrutinize each envelope for stamps that the post office machines had failed to mark as used. The two employees confessed that they recovered several perfectly good stamps this way each day, but failed to see the cost-effectiveness of paying them to fish out a handful of 32 cent stamps, even bearing in mind their embarrassingly low wages.

After I felt I had made myself quite valuable to the company, I wrote them a letter implying that I would resign if I were not given a substantial raise. I was quite nervous about this bit of brinksmanship, especially after Mrs. Golden called me into her office.

"That's a fine Monet print, Mrs. Golden," I said, indicating the *Water Lilies* behind her desk.

"Thank you. Sit down."

I sat down on a metal folding chair. I could tell visitors didn't sit in her office for long.

"That was a fine letter you wrote. And I hear you are doing a good job."

"Thank you."

"We would like to offer you a raise of 10 cents an hour. What do you say?"

I was shocked by this low-balling.

"How about 50 cents per hour?"

"No, I'm sorry. We can't do that."

"But I've edited four books this month. And I've written new computer programs to fully automate the build of your electronic products!"

"I'll give you 25 cents an hour. But really: no more. You're very young. You'll make more when you're older."

I was proud to have wheedled even this raise out of the Goldens. Others didn't feel that a showdown with Mrs. Golden was worth it.

"Besides," many of them said, "I won't be here much longer."

But everyone's failure to escape was especially acute around Christmas time. I'm sure people were even drafting their New Year's resolutions, and

"Find New Job" had to have been an even more pressing resolution for many than "Quit Smoking."

Luckily, I only spent one Christmas there. Mrs. Golden was very excited about our Christmas party. She bought a "big sandwich" which she placed in our lunchroom. But we still were not granted more than our standard half-hour for lunch. An array of wrapped gifts sat on another table. When my curiosity got the better of me, I opened one small package to find a coffee mug filled with small chocolates. Merry Christmas.

Years after I left, I heard that the Goldens had started providing a Christmas lunch at a Chinese restaurant. One employee who had the temerity to give his notice a few days before the Christmas party was actually denied entry into the Chinese restaurant despite his four years' service to the Goldens.

The Goldens themselves only recognized Yom Kippur. Despite working on Saturday, the Jewish Sabbath, all year, and displaying not the slightest shred of piety, they observed Yom Kippur without fail. They were probably hedging their bets about the whole God thing. So for one day their empire ran itself without direction. How it must have galled them, even as they sat in synagogue, to think about us slacking off, chattering to each other, perhaps stealing pencils. It was impossible to imagine the Goldens praying, whether singly or in concert, to imagine that they acknowledged any higher power.

During the last few months of my employment with the Goldens, there was increasing talk about their handing the business over to their son, Brice. Brice was the middle of their three sons. The older son was up north, running the New York branch of the family business. The youngest son was apparently a spectacularly successful corporate lawyer, who had earned the undying awe of his parents by renouncing his inheritance. He wasn't on particularly bad terms with the family, and would occasionally do some legal consulting for them. He had made his own fortune, and so he didn't have to waste his days in the Golden compound—perhaps a "sick" building by OSHA standards—worrying about second-rate legal manuals.

Not that Brice's assumption of the Goldens' Florida empire required much effort on his part. Brice frequently arrived around 10:00 a.m. and was known to leave around 4:00 p.m. We knew that Mrs. Golden supervised the personnel aspects of the business, and Mr. Golden the technical aspects (watching Mr. Golden sweat before a DOS prompt and type incorrect commands gave us all pleasure), but what was Brice's role?

We received some clue as to how Brice spent the day after he bought a new computer. Brice gave his old computer to John, one of the editors, who happened to be a little more internet-savvy than most for the time. Out of curiosity, John checked the computer's internet images cache, and found that Brice had maxed out his hard drive by failing to delete his temporary internet files. That's probably the whole reason Brice thought he needed a new computer. John called a bunch of us to check out the images in the cache. John laughed gleefully, pointing out the "See Brad Pitt Nude!" images and the like that had filled up Brice's hard-drive. Nobody knew Brice was gay.

Later, we heard about Brice's lovers from the Goldens' housekeeper, whom they occasionally sent over to clean their publishing compound. The time-honored servant grapevine began to work (we were "the help" too), and Shelley, the mousy maid, told us all about the wild, all-male parties Brice threw at the house.

Shelley also told us that Mrs. Golden was a fiendish hotel-soap collector, and devoted several shelves in a closet to her myriad collection of bar soap. Mrs. Golden instructed Shelley to bring the hotel soap to Brice's or to the publishing compound whenever supplies ran low.

Suddenly I understood why there were so many brands kinds of bar soap in the men's room.

Fridays at the Blind Pig's Pub

As I speed over the muddy roads, my dashboard lights flicker, signifying power loss. I am conscious of my car as an island of civilization in the sub-tropical forest. If I break down, or get stuck in the mud, I imagine being found first by a marauding bear rather than the passing car of a helpful neighbor. Most likely I would be rescued by one of the pickup-truck-driving senior citizens to whom I've taught Sunday school a few times.

The thought of all this makes me lean on the gas pedal, plunging my rusted out '77 Cadillac into mud holes with greater impact, praying that the back tires will continue to grab the mud somehow.

I imagine my car's complete loss of power and the subsequent rescue scene vividly: the 80 year-old "mayor" of the trailer park, Lucy, shaking her head sadly at my car; the tow truck's headlights shining on the ugly black letters that spelled out "Fuck You, Whore!"; the police coming to arrest me for driving around with a profanity written on my car.

My father, or perhaps one of his girlfriend-proxies, had spray-painted the black letters on the white-vinyl top a few years before, back when it belonged to my mother during their divorce. Later, I drove the rusty-burgundy Fuck-You-Whore Caddy down from Cleveland, and now drive it around central Florida, including in the trailer park—mainly senior and religious—where I live in my deceased grandmother's mobile home, and even attend church and Sunday school sometimes.

Secretly I'm an atheist, but my grandmother's friends gave me a key to the church, and let me use the piano there, so there are some benefits to hiding my atheism. Church is the one place I am completely bored, and this boredom allows me to relax.

I gingerly pull the Caddy out of the mud roads, and onto the first paved road of my route, Florida State Route 42. I accelerate and look once again at the broken speedometer, before adjusting my speed on instinct alone. It is only ten miles into the town of Deland, the county seat of Volusia County, Florida, close to Daytona. It's Friday night at eight o'clock and no one else is on the road.

I creep into Deland, park behind the police station, and walk in the rain toward The Blind Pig's Pub. It's a hangout for local Stetson University students, an island of bohemia in a sleepy Florida town. Folk musicians play there sometimes, even neo-grunge bands, and it smells like patchouli inside. The Blind Pig's Pub is named after a Prohibition-era speak-easy, the blindness referring to the policemen's bribe-induced blindness to its selling alcohol.

I am very self-conscious, and sort of nervously clench my body as I enter, hoping the place is already full and I won't be noticed as an obvious sad loner. It's about 8:30 p.m. when I enter, and The Blind Pig's Pub is still nearly empty.

Aside from a few patrons sitting at the bar, there is only the usual insolent bartender and Jeannie, the object of my desire, who waves a greeting from afar. Perhaps she remembers me from last Friday, or the Friday before. I nod back weakly, as if people don't remember other people, as if this is my first time here. Although I will sit and pine after her for the next several hours, I'm not happy that she knows me, and can probably sense my loneliness.

Jeannie has long, straight, sandy hair, Siamese-green eyes, and a knowing smile. She usually dresses all in white: a white blouse, white short-shorts and white sneakers without socks. She is short, tan everywhere, full-figured and friendly. She serves beer energetically, and walks rhythmically, as if some happy tune is ever playing in her head: Jeannie's song. She seems confident her fate will not be that of a lifer barmaid.

This thought cheers me up as well. I sit at a table in the corner, and open the book I brought. I had purposefully left *King Lear* back in the trailer park and brought along a book of popular fiction that I thought might interest Jeannie. I also take out the notebook I carry around with me to signal to people that I am a writer. Somehow I think that the "right" kind of woman will be impressed by this, rather than find it totally fucking pathetic that I carry a book and notebook out with me on a Friday night.

Jeannie approaches my table.

"Hey there. How you doing? What are you reading?"

"It's called *American Tabloid*. It's a novel about the Kennedy assassination. Great book."

"It sounds like it, like that movie *JFK*. You should let me borrow it when you're done. I'm almost done with my book."

"OK. Yeah, I will," I say hesitantly. I leave a weird pause in the air. It doesn't quite occur to me fast enough that lending her a book can be a small step toward building a relationship. Nor do I even think to ask her a follow-up question about what she likes to read. I am nervous, and excited by her presence, and cannot think of a thing to say. I am perhaps two years older than her, but feel myself to be almost of a different generation.

"So what can I get you?"

I order the cheapest beer, unwilling to invest even an extra 25 cents per bottle for a "good" brand like Bud Lite. I'm proud to have not made the hackneyed quip about Milwaukee's worst. When she flashes her full, yet lop-sided, smile, I don't feel so bad about my obvious poverty. She walks to the bar, and my eyes follow her movements. As she fills a beer-glass from the tap, I begin scribbling gibberish in my notebook so that she'll catch me writing when she returns.

Jeannie's back in no time.

"What are you writing?" she asks.

"Oh, I'm just taking notes for my *novel*." I let the last word hang in the air impressively. "It's not very good though."

"I'm sure it's fine," she says.

"No. I'm not very good yet. I've got a lot to learn."

"Awwww....you'll get there," Jeannie says sympathetically, leaning down and hugging my head against her chest, almost maternally. I am electrified by this gesture, but suspicious. I'm sure that she doesn't really like me, that she is just angling for a good tip. She will certainly get one, despite my poverty and unemployment. But I really don't know what to make of it. Perhaps a vestigial Southern hospitality? She smells freshly showered. I am grateful to feel my desire for her. I can hardly speak, but I should be saying something smooth.

She steps back, and says "See you later," a little wanly, and then attends to another table that has just filled up.

I am hesitant to approach the young women in this bar, most of whom appear to be college age, or just older. I am 25, out of college for three years, and feel worthless for not yet being a Contributing Member of Society. I feel like a dirty old man ogling younger college women. Everyone else around me seems improbably hip to me.

I drink beers and smoke and pretend to read and write. Before I know it, I have drunk five beers, and the room has grown crowded and loud. I feel I cannot monopolize one of Jeannie's tables anymore. I collect my things, and find a lone barstool to squeeze into.

The guy on the barstool to my right strikes up a conversation with me. I take him for a friendly Good Old Country Boy sort. He's drunk as a Pope.

I fix my gaze straight ahead to avoid any prolonged exchange.

"What's your problem?"

"Huh?"

"Don't you like country folk?"

"Sure. I live in the country myself."

"Uh huh. All your life, right?" he says sarcastically. "Where're you really from? Chicago?"

"Cleveland," I say.

"Same difference."

"How about you?"

"Why?" he says suspiciously.

"I'm just talking, man."

"Southern Florida," he says grudgingly. "I'm a writer. I write movies."

"Really? What have you written?"

"Well, most of the scripts haven't been made, you see. —And I'm working on one now called *Glades*. But the one that got made was called *Red Dawn*. J'ever see that?"

"*Red Dawn*! You wrote *Red Dawn*?"

"Yes, sir."

The moment is surreal: I'm looking at a gaunt, somewhat angry-looking South Floridian, who claims to have written *Red Dawn*.

I had watched *Red Dawn* more than once on cable television as an impressionable adolescent. One morning Russian paratroopers land in Colorado while simultaneously Soviet and Cuban forces invade from Mexico. All of America west of the Mississippi is quickly overrun by Communist forces. But Patrick Swayze and C. Thomas Howell form a guerilla outfit of high school kids called The Wolverines, who camp out, drink ritualistic deer blood, and blow up a lot of Russian tanks. The Russians are soon more focused on finding those pesky Wolverines than in defeating the U.S. Army, dug in yet supine on the eastern bank of the Mississippi. *Red Dawn* was made during the Reagan Paranoia phase of the Cold War, and was a critical and financial failure, but has since become a cult favorite for people who just can't wait for the day when they finally get to use their guns on all the annoying people around them.

"*Red Dawn*? The one where the Russians invade America? And those high school kids become guerillas? What'd they call themselves?"

"The Wolverines."

"Right. Wolverines. Wow. Yeah, I'm a writer too, but don't think I can write for the screen just yet, because I'm not familiar enough with the medium: all those camera angles, close-ups, panning, low shots; plus lighting and blocking. There's simply too much to know."

"That's all there is to it. What are you? A cinematographer? All you need is a good story. I'm now working on a new movie called *Glades*." He takes a large swig.

"It's kind of like *Karate Kid* meets *Glades*."

I nod understandingly. "*Glades* meets *Glades*. But it hasn't been made. Yet. Got it."

Now he's giving me the pitch, but I can hardly hear him. My body language is turned slightly away, as if I might need to flee any second. And The Blind Pig is now as packed as a factory farm, and so loud I can't isolate words very well.

Glades seems to be about a woman who lives in Florida's Everglades, and teaches a lonely man how to live in the wilderness. Her son from a previous marriage also learns life's lessons. Then the boy's mother dies violently. And soon some more people die. And then some more. He's not the author of *Red Dawn* for nothing.

I've sat listening for some time now, and I see trust reflected in his eyes.

"I've seen things a man never ought to see!" he shouts at me. He shouts something about a bomb or 'Nam.

I imagine him cracking up before my eyes. I stop to consider that there are probably at least a few concealed firearms in this very Floridian bar, yet I myself am not packing any heat. The self-proclaimed *Red Dawn* screenwriter must have at least one firearm. And now he is fighting back tears. Does that make everyone more safe or less?

"My wife died some years back. There was this terrible accident..." He stares into my eyes so intensely that the sanctity of my thoughts feels violated. I imagine that he has the eyes of a murderer, though TV is my only frame of reference for such judgments. I do not understand what he is saying. The noise of the crowded bar now drowns out his voice.

I sense he is confessing everything to me. I nod feebly, vapidly, as though I understand, but I can hear nothing. He feels responsible for his wife's death. Perhaps he is confessing killing her to me right now, but I can't tell for sure.

"She's in a better place. It's OK. Everything's fine now," he tells me when he's finished, even shaking my fear-frozen hand.

"Yes, it is," I say, stepping off the barstool to escape. "Good luck with *Glades*," I say, and walk away.

"*Glades!*" he shouts, as if chanting "Semper Fi!"

I lose myself in the crowd and find a stool at the other end of the bar. I am a little shaken by my conversation with the screenwriter, and only want to collect myself. Jeannie smiles at me, and brings another beer. I am revived by the sight of her, and my eyes follow her white-clad form greedily. I watch her serve others with a comparable friendliness, and decide she isn't particularly interested in me.

An older man on the barstool to my left greets me with a nod. Floridians are very friendly.

We get to talking. I probably sound as though I am interrogating him, ascertaining his motives for visiting a college bar. Perhaps he is a dirty old man, or a professor. Or both.

He is Jack: a large man in his fifties wearing a sport jacket and cowboy boots, and sporting a silver-gray pony-tail.

"So what do you do, Jack?" I ask, expecting to hear a tale of failure.

"I'm an artist." Pride drips off his last word like fat melting off a spit.

"So you make good money at that?" I ask, still fishing for a tale of woe.

"Actually. Yes." And Jack smiles a shit-eating grin, and takes a long swallow from his frosted beer mug.

"What kind of artist?"

"A sculptor. But it's not all about exhibitions. I also designs sets for theaters, and do some graphic art. I used to think I had to become Rodin or nothing. But eventually I made my peace with the world, and found a way to do what I love and make a living. I mean, I even got a boat."

"But don't you feel that you've shamelessly sold out?" I ask, trying to shock him with candor.

"No."

I order another beer. I am now in a dangerous drunken state in which I feel that everything I say is interesting. Now I am telling Jack about God. How there isn't one. I am constructing elaborate verbal catapults with which to assail the fortress of religion.

Jack shakes his head like all this palaver is unnecessary.

"We're all gods in a way," he intones. I glare at him dubiously. "No, I mean it," he says. "You can't tell me that the universe is an accident. Things happen for a reason. And if you open yourself up to certain psychic channels, good things can happen to you." Jack segues to first person, and spins me a yarn.

"Years ago I was completely broke, and needed $500 to pay the rent, or else I would be evicted. I had no friends or family to turn to. But then, like a flash, I hear in my mind: 5314237," he says prophetically to me, impressed with himself that he still remembers the numbers.

"So I bought a Lottery ticket, Pick 3, for the numbers 531. I won 500 dollars. The next day, I play a Pick 4, 10,000 dollar jackpot. I played 4237, but the number came up 4236. Can you believe that?

"Why did the psychic powers let you down when it was big-money time?"

"I got too greedy about it. The point is I got just the money I needed at a critical juncture in my life."

"So your belief in higher powers is based on a winning lottery number? *Lots* of people think they hear numbers, you know. And most of them lose. It's the fallacy of the positive instance. You just got lucky," I say brightly, lifting my glass to his fortune.

"You don't understand." He says as if I'm hopeless, and takes another drink. He starts talking about Carlos Castaneda, and obtaining spiritual allies to aid one's endeavors. Jack can tell he's lost me. I smile, imagining a business book called "Don Carlos: Shaman, CEO."

My eyes wander about for something more interesting, and land on a young woman standing behind Jack.

She's a fucking dead ringer for Nathalie, my true love, the one who crushed me forever, who just got married two months ago: lush black hair, hazel eyes, full parted lips, great legs. Dead ringer. Not fair. I gawk too long, and she says: "What?" playfully, as if she had known me her whole life and we were resuming some earlier conversation.

I step off my barstool, nodding good-bye to Jack, the successful artist.

She's still looking for an explanation for my staring at her and touches her face self-consciously, seeking a wart or some other flaw.

"Hi, I'm Dan." My superego has finally dissolved in the beer. But I'm too slow-witted to just blurt out that she's gorgeous, though it's running through my head. I extend my hand.

"Susanna." She takes my hand and in her hand I feel the energy of a higher-order being. She's plastered, but her eyes shine beatifically.

"I'm a special education teacher. Department head, actually." She looks 25 to me, at the most.

"You want a job?" she asks me absurdly. "Because I can get you a job."

I'm momentarily tempted, but I shrug. "No thanks." I'm not ready to face a 9 to 5 job. I still have almost 300 dollars in the bank, and I'm not paying rent.

"It's better than working at Disney. And I *love* my students."

Then this guy stands behind her, rubbing her shoulders, squeezing her arms, then ribcage, standing close-in behind. I'm mad with jealousy. Oddly, his touches elicit no response from her. I find it disquieting to watch. She's too drunk or too jaded to care. Does she just assume that this is what guys in bars do? Or is it that she feels liberated by allowing it, even if she's not really interested? She must know him.

I nearly burst out laughing as she keeps telling me trivial things while the guy gropes her with intent, but still tries to seem just like a cool bar guy about it. I'm ready to see him cup her breasts with his hands right there in the bar.

"Are you guys married?" I ask.

"To him?" she laughs. "I just met him like twenty minutes ago."

"Oh, I'm sorry," I say, wondering how he managed to acquire such intimate privileges within twenty minutes.

"Well, *I'm* married," interjects the guy, sneering cavalierly about his present attempt at infidelity. He steps out from behind Susanna and extends his hand to me.

"Hey guy. I'm Dylan." He is tall and thin, and wears an open Hawaiian shirt. He claims to be the manager of the Cafe D'Vinci, another recently opened night spot in Deland.

"Three short months ago there was *nothing* in Deland. But now we have The Blind Pig's Pub, the Cafe D'Vinci, and that fascist sports bar."

"The one with the good chicken wings?"

"Right. But D'Vinci is great, man. We got alternative bands every Saturday. Come tomorrow! Poetry readings. Babes."

Three lovely young women join us and talk to Susanna all at the same time.

I begin talking to them. I lie about having inherited a house and some money, when the truth is I inherited $400 in savings bonds from my grandmother and now live in her mobile home.

"Guess what I do," asks the short blonde with fragile blue eyes encased in her glasses.

"Teacher."

"Right!" She titters with the joy of recognition.

The other one looks tired and overworked at 23.

"You're medical, right? A nurse?"

Correct again. They look at each other impressed. How did I know?

I mumble that I'm a writer, implying some special insight into humanity. But my guesses were in reality just blind luck.

Seeing Susanna occupied, I turn my attention to Laura, the blonde algebra teacher. She is blue-eyed, red-lipped fresh, and laughs at all the right places. Just as I catch her attention, another one, Joy, interjects:

"Laura! But what about that great guy from the *other place*? What's his name?" Joy has the aura of a British witch, perhaps in the Stevie Nicks tradition. Joy introduces herself to me as an "entrepreneur." She runs Merlin's Place, a New Age shop full of crystals, esoteric literature, and whatnot, just around the corner. I promise to pay her a visit, as if I have disposable income.

Dylan has been working his way around, managing to stop and give each of the women some shallow bar cheer, and a brief shoulder massage. They all shrug him off as an obvious pest, except for Susanna who still doesn't fend off his advances at all for some reason, as if they are not really happening.

"That guy is a little too grabby," the nurse tells Susanna, while Dylan goes to the bathroom. "You should like this guy better. He's a gentleman," she says, pointing at me. Susanna smiles, breaking my heart, and then indifferently stuffs three mozzarella sticks in her mouth.

I shrug off the gentleman label. "I'm as much a pig as any man."

And in just a few minutes they must leave. It's almost 2:00 a.m., and the bar-staff is starting to corral us out the door.

Laura at least says: "I hope to see you again, Dan."

I'm too slow-witted or scared to even ask for her phone number. I am crestfallen at my own indecision.

Susanna refuses to leave with her friends. Instead, she leaves with Dylan five minutes later, saying "Bye" to me as if she'll see me next time.

I stay to finish my beer, pausing to reflect upon how completely inept I am at being single. I watch Jeannie, barmaid of my dreams, being ogled and handled by patrons at another table. I leave The Blind Pig's Pub just before 2:00 a.m., having ordered a final beer that I smuggle out by holding my notebook up in front of the bottle.

I am outside walking empty streets, absurdly carrying a beer, a notebook, and *American Tabloid*. I feel alone, convinced that everyone else at The Blind Pig will effortlessly hook up with someone that night, while I am comparatively defective, unable to accept that it all comes down to physical attractiveness rather than...what exactly did I have to offer? Literary pretension? Might as well have brought fucking *King Lear*. I am trying to find the Café D'Vinci. Why?

When I find it, it still looks a lot like the furniture store that it was four months ago.

I go inside. The bar is dark and empty; closing time. Dylan, Susanna and—to my great surprise— Jack, the boat-owning psychic sculptor lottery winner, are sitting at a round table with vodka-and-cranberries before them. Dylan has one of his hands on Susanna at all times—knee, thigh, arm, shoulder—while the three of them engage in three one-on-one conversations.

I stand at the bar and am served by a young lady with blonde dreadlocks. "Last call."

I hold up one finger, as if I need a moment. She slides a superfluous beer to me, searches my face for exactly two seconds, and then she writes **Not Interested** in a steno notebook lying open on the bar.

"Who's not interested?" I ask.

She scratches it out without looking up.

"*Who?*"

"I don't want to talk about it. That's why I crossed it out," she challenges.

I begin wondering whether *she* was not interested in me, or whether she thought *I* was not interested in her, or whether she was writing about something else entirely. Another writer. I glance at her notebook. There are no other such observations written on that page, so maybe she isn't in the habit of recording observations of each patron, or evaluating the potential of every man in her path. I look at her now, wondering whether I am interested in her. With her blonde dreadlocks and tan skin she looks like she originates from some remote galaxy of cool that I will only ever read about. She strikes me as if she's wearing a costume, like she really is someone else entirely. I am very drunk and consciously stare at a wall, only to stop looking at her.

"Thank you, Barmaid Who Writes Things Down," I manage to say. She looks disappointed to me.

From her table, Susanna catches my attention, and waves me over, like an old casual friend. I head over to the table, hearing her finishing a story.

"And so it's all my asshole step-father's fault."

I join the others at table. I put down the beer I just ordered. I do not want it; I am dry and drunk and sluggish, almost hung-over already. But I drink the beer anyway, because I do not want the night to end.

Dylan is now describing his glorious establishment for us, pointing at memorabilia on the walls, recounting the 'history' of the Cafe D'Vinci, now open for three glorious months.

No one is listening.

Only the four of us are left in the room. Susanna rises in the middle of Dylan's story and goes up to the bar. As she stands at the bar, waiting for the now-vanished barmaid to serve her, Dylan approaches her. He stands behind her and begins rubbing her shoulders, her back, her legs, and gradually her ass, groping her beyond any decorum. Susanna rests her head on the bar, on the verge of passing out.

Jack watches this casually.

I walk out of the bar, feeling like an unclean voyeur and moral coward. But was I supposed to beat him up? What was happening in there?

Outside in the cool night, rain falling now, light and steady, I find my rusty old Cadillac and climb in, blind drunk. I don't want to drive home drunk, but there are no cabs in Deland, Florida, and no money in my wallet. I don't have a choice. At least there is no traffic.

I ease the Caddy out from behind the police station, wishing I had stayed home and written. I leave the windows about half-way down to suck in cold air, and accelerate into the night. I play a cassette and smoke, but the cherry flies off, landing on my shirt, then my pants, and finally the down-to-sponge upholstery of my beater, where I snuff it out with my index finger.

I turn right onto the muddy dirt road, relieved that I have at least eluded the police, who never patrol the dirt roads. I keep skidding in that mud, but continue on doggedly. Perhaps I will be shot by a stray bullet from one of the hunters from the lodges down the side roads I have never traversed. I see a car up ahead in my headlights, parked alongside the road with its lights off. I pass slowly to see if anyone is there, afraid to stop entirely, lest I get stuck. No one's there, but someone's hapless 4-cylinder Buick hatch-back is embedded in the mud. An ominous sign. Someone must have rescued the driver but left the car for the night. Not many more seniors will still be out joyriding at 2:25 a.m. though. But the Caddy has real power—472 engine block, 4 barrel carb. The engine whirs reliably.

I park the car in the driveway, get out and look up at the planetarium-dark sky, the bright stars. A cow bellows from the farm across the sand road, and I think I hear some pigs grunting in the mud. I imagine the poisonous snakes that could be crawling around in my yard, or my back porch, or even inside the mobile home.

I lay in bed on the cool sheets, in reverie over Nathalie and then Susanna. I lack the wherewithal to conquer them. Nathalie is already married off, back in Cleveland. I lack money and resources. I live in a mobile home. My social status is null. I could well live my whole life alone.

My eyes well up with the thought of lonely life, but it warms up my face, and some tears come before I pass out in the bed.

Last Night in Deerwood

The night before I left Deerwood, Florida, I went to say good-bye to Bill and Lucy, distant cousins of mine and Deerwood elders. Secretly I was weary at the thought of seeing them one last time, but I felt I ought to, for decency's sake. Maybe they would let me play their piano a bit.

Hell, two years ago, upon my arrival in Deerwood, when I was downtrodden and perilously close to a full relapse into Christianity, I had seen them frequently, and they had treated me as a kind, intelligent, church-going (if under-employed) asset to the community. Lucy described me as the "flower of Deerwood," much to my mortification. Imagine for a young man like myself to be christened so!

It was about 8:00 p.m., and I was exhausted from helping Sally pack all her earthly belongings into the moving van for our big move to Washington, DC. When I finally found love in Florida our first impulse was to get the hell out and get real jobs up north.

#

Oh well. This won't take long. I rang the bell at Bill and Lucy's.

"There he is!" exclaimed Bill, as he opened the door.

"I thought you were going to leave without saying goodbye!" cried Lucy, about fifty pounds heavier than when I met her two years ago. Bill is quite fond of making "black cows" (ice cream with chocolate syrup) for her, and yet abstains from them himself, as if he is fattening her up for some sinister purpose. I imagine some mysterious cannibalistic religious cult that Bill belongs to, perhaps already hiding out in the woods near Deerwood.

"Of course, I came to say good-bye," I said, syrup dripping from my words. My effort at playing the penitent prodigal son was palpably unconvincing. I eyed their piano in one corner of the room and the clock in the other.

Their first order of business was to assure me that they would "look after" my great Aunt Mae and Uncle Myron who still lived around the corner.

"We all are *very concerned* about them," said Lucy. "They're not getting any younger you know. But we'll take care of them. Won't we, Bill?"

Lucy herself will need looking after pretty soon. She is 75 and has mysterious, epileptic-type fits that even the learned doctors at the expensive clinic were unable to diagnose or treat. ("You need to rest more," was all they could offer her after six weeks on a waiting list and a battery of tests.) I had witnessed two of these fits first hand. Her neck drooped like a wet chicken, and a thin stream of saliva ran out of her mouth.

Bill is 82, happy, and remarkably well-preserved. He takes good care of himself. Bill is of a technical bent, having been an engineer for McDonnell Douglas until twenty years ago.

But Lucy definitely wears the pants in the family. She is, after all, the Mayor of Deerwood, population 120, about half of whom are nominally RLDS (Reorganization Church of Jesus Christ of Latter Day Saints), a small, neo-Mormon religious denomination.

I was RLDS as a kid. But when I was twelve everyone in my family became born-again Christians. Now I'm an atheist, but I keep this to myself in Deerwood. I've even taught Sunday school to the seniors.

Lucy is going on about my great-aunt and uncle.

"I've already been in contact with Mae and Myron's doctors and with Human Services about their situation. Frankly, I think it's time that Myron gave up his driver's license. He might hurt someone!"

I vividly remember the last time Myron drove me to town, his palsied hands on the wheel liable to lose control and plow the car into oncoming traffic at any moment.

Aunt Mae, for her part, had given up the idea of driving after she drove the car into a Deerwood ditch a few months back. She's too small to see over the steering wheel; passers-by were sure her vehicle was unoccupied. ("The Rapture?" they must have wondered.) But she keeps her license, and still asserts that she could drive in a pinch.

Myron, however, has no intention of giving up his license. To rob Myron of his independence—a man's man who had weathered the Great Depression and The War, cared for legions of family members, as well as faithfully served his church, his Deerwood community, and his brother Shriners—was tantamount to killing him.

"Yeah, it's really a hard decision to make," I tell Bill and Lucy. "But I think if you get the government involved, or do too much for them, I think they'll stop trying. It's just not their style. I think they want to go out in full harness."

Lucy nods profoundly, placating me, knowing that I will soon be out of the picture and so my opinion is now meaningless.

I had already discussed the issue of Mae and Myron with all the leading families of Deerwood, including my other distant cousins. I was able to share my (pointless, abstract) wonderment at the complexity of such an issue again with Lucy and Bill.

"Just like we ask ourselves at what point young people are mature and *independent* enough to drive, vote, marry, raise children, die for their country, so we face the similar issues later in life: just when *are* we too old to do x, y, and z? Myron and Mae have exercised their independence for a long time; you seek to take what is theirs."

Bill and Lucy have no use for such abstractions, I can tell. I keep reminding myself that they too are old, and that I should in no way suggest the limited powers of old people to their faces. But then: why are they going after my great-aunt and uncle?

Fifteen minutes have passed; I feel justified in winding down my visit. I slouch in the easy chair like an old man, ready for his evening nap.

"So what are you going to do with the mobile home?" asks Lucy, conversationally.

"Huh? My Mom *thought* of renting it, but it's really in no condition to be rented. I mean part of the floor in the back porch is very weak. And—well, you never know what kind of renters you get. I doubt if I could find anyone anyway. So I'm just going to leave it where it is. We'll stay there when we come to visit."

Lucy's voice contracts now; she speaks conspiratorially. "I know someone who would rent it."

My heart sinks. I think I can sense what is coming. I blink blankly, my mind sluggish in apprehending this shocking development.

"Joe and Wendy have had such a hard time," she says. "And yesterday they had to leave their home. They're living in their *car* right now. Can you believe it? And it would be so *wonderful* if they could have another chance." She sighs loudly, no doubt in wonderment at the wonderfulness of Joe and Wendy's big chance to live in my mother's mobile home.

Her last statement is a prompt; I simply have to say something. But all I can do is blink idiotically, vaguely feeling that the role of coincidence in my life has been large enough to suggest a Dickens novel.

I look at Bill who is wearing this You'll Do The Right Thing, Son expression.

The Cranes? I am thinking. *Naw. Not the Cranes.*

The Cranes are Deerwood's official poor folk: a ne'er-do-well family that through a staggering series of blunders and indecisions has managed to be booted out of three Deerwood domiciles already. They moved up to Central Florida after Hurricane Andrew wiped them out. They somehow landed in Deerwood soon after, an arrival that Lucy once attributed to divine providence.

"Isn't it wonderful?" she had crooned, visions of the right hand of the Lord dancing before her. I shrugged, then and still unable to find the wonder in it all. I am still stupefied that they managed to *find* Deerwood. How did they hear about it? They had neither friends, relations or ties to the church. Why were they there?

No, it wasn't so wonderful. Out of sheer pity, a comfortable Deerwood widower had rented them his spare triple-wide mobile home, some two years before.

Joe and Wendy Crane, along with their two daughters, Christine, a 15 year old trollop, and Beth, 12, probably the most sensible and educated of the bunch, arrived in Deerwood. They rode in Joe's bright red Camaro, which Hurricane Andrew had miraculously spared.

At first everything seemed fine. Joe found a job in a quarry or something (though who ever heard of a quarry in Florida?), an hour's drive away. Maybe even less in the sports car. It was an "honest" (i.e., low-paying) job. Wendy was confident that she could again make $14 an hour cleaning houses, just as she claimed she did in Miami.

But they just couldn't make ends meets. Stories of their $300 electric bills began to circulate. Early-rising neighbors reported that the TV and lights were left on all night. The air-conditioner blasted 24 hours per day despite some visibly open windows.

Wendy, perhaps incognizant of just how far from *everything* Deerwood is, never found the counted-on cleaning job. Nor any other job. She was finally offered cleaning work from a disabled Deerwood widow, but at a modest wage; and she refused. One day, the bright red Camaro disappeared—hocked, or perhaps repossessed; nobody knows for sure. It was replaced by a battered, red pickup truck.

And then, at Bill and Lucy's suggestion, the Cranes began attending church. After a few weeks, Bill, while giving the Sunday sermon, reached out to the people's hearts, beseeching them to give to a special fund for the good family Crane, who were suddenly sitting in the front pew that week, looking very religious. The daughters both wore plain smock dresses of the same cut. Joe Crane's Sunday best consisted of boots, jeans and dress-shirt.

Truly, thought the good people of Deerwood, this is a family in need. Bill reminded them that the Lord repays us one-hundred fold for our alms. Some church folk gave cheerfully. At one-hundred fold, God is a better investment than the Dow.

But it wouldn't be the last time the good people of Deerwood were called upon to come to the Crane's succor. Wendy, soon after, was pregnant again.

"And these kids" (Lucy always calls Joe and Wendy "kids" because they are only in their 40s) "don't even have money for baby clothes."

Joe bows his head somberly, vaguely evoking Job and others who have endured unjust fates at the hands of the cosmos.

So Joe and his family kept coming to church; the girls always wore the same dresses. Joe wore the same jeans and boots. Wendy grew bigger with child. Joe is then routinely called upon to "usher," to help pass around the collection plate. All eyes watched him like a hawk as he handled the plate full of money.

Joe's battered red pickup truck, which he drove 45 miles to work each way every day despite its inability to go in reverse, collapsed one day in ruin in his oil- and transmission-fluid-stained driveway.

"Certainly," proclaimed Bill to the congregation, "a man must have a way to work, to support his wife and children." A special collection was taken, the whole family summoned to the front of the sanctuary, their heads lowered in prayer, or in humiliation, and the Deerwood Community bought Joe a used car for $600.

Meanwhile, the kindly widower landlord had finally had it with the Cranes. The rent was many months in arrears. He booted them out.

Then they miraculously moved-on-up to a *bona fide* Deerwood house. They even had high hopes of purchasing it. This too did not work out. The rent alone proved to be higher than Joe's net salary.

This was about a year ago. I had volunteered to help them move. Their next destination was to be yet another house, two blocks away, owned by a Miami couple, who planned to retire there in five years or so. But they were happy to rent it for a while. To a nice family anyway. Lucy told them that the Cranes were very nice.

Moving day with the Cranes was to prove my most intimate contact with them. I had no idea why I had decided to help them. Lucy probably asked me.

The house they were vacating, Crane-occupied for only about six months, contained a truly astounding volume and variety of bric-a-brac. I noticed a fine CD stereo player, a VCR, a TV (either very new or *rented*—another cash hemorrhage), and a tri-pod telescope in heaps on the floor, its delicate lens perilously close to a forgotten darning needle.

The daughters trod carelessly on the object-strewn floor, sometimes crunching things underfoot as they went. Many new things—pointlessly and thoughtlessly bought because they were only $5 or $10 or $20 dollars—filled their environs. The girls had very full closets of clothes, but where were these clothes on Sunday? Why the humble frocks?

Disney videos littered the floor everywhere. Their refrigerator had been stocked with overpriced packaged and processed foods: munchies, ice-cream treats, processed MSG-laden food. *Don't they know raw foodstuffs are cheaper?* I am thinking. I check out Joe's record collection. Beatles, Pink Floyd, Led Zeppelin: the latter two groups incriminating evidence that he smokes pot, or used to.

Wait a minute, I think. *Am I going to be judgmental about that? What's happening to me?* I grab another box and throw it on the truck.

The Cranes are polite enough, and ask me a little more about myself.

"What do you do? How do you like Deerwood? Who are you related to?"

"Everyone," I can only answer, "is somehow my 6th cousin."

The girls ask whether I have children, an idea I thought was fantastic.

"How old do you think I am?" I ask, surprised.

"I don't know, 37?" guesses the trollop.

I laugh, feeling my high forehead. "I'm only 25," I implore.

Wendy is apologetic. "She's just a girl. She doesn't know." Is "she" too young, or the wrong gender, to understand? What kind of message are they sending these girls?

But this move too, did not work out for the Cranes. Despite the generous rental agreement, the rent could not be paid. Perhaps in part because the Cranes, inexplicably, had purchased a satellite dish capable of delivering 100 TV channels. After it's paid for, it's only a dollar a day, they must have reasoned.

And yesterday, they had been evicted from that domicile as well.

#

Bill and Lucy are looking at me, waiting for my response to their proposal of dumping the Cranes into my mother's rusty mobile home. Instead of assessing the dubious character of these renters, I had spent the moment thinking of what a boon this could be for my mother. Instead of having to pay $700 per year in property taxes and insurance for nothing, she could actually derive a profit from the decrepit mobile home! But wait. These were the Cranes. If it sounds too good to be true...

"Well, I'd have to talk to my mother. It's *her* property."

"You want to call her right now?" Lucy offers the cordless phone to me.

"How much do you think your mother would want to rent it for?" asks Bill.

"Uh. I don't know. You see, I'm leaving tomorrow and now is not—"

"Oh we could take care of *everything*," says Lucy. "And it would help them *so much*."

"We could draw up a contract," says Bill, "that would make them responsible for all of the utilities. Joe is very handy. He could fix your mother's porch, or anything else that goes wrong."

And so on. By now, in an almost delirious condition from two days of frantic activity, my mind kicks into high gear again.

Gee, somebody moving in. So many arrangements to be made! So much to do! What should I do? How can I help?

Heavens knows why, but I felt eager to show Bill and Lucy my altruistic credentials after a year of absence from church.

I begin taking notes, playing the responsible man-of-affairs, asking questions about insurance, utilities, security, contracts, and lawyers, all of which I am largely ignorant of. They have an answer for everything. I am still only yearning to play their piano. I won't have access to a piano at all in DC.

I have to leave though. Lucy exudes her "love" for me, which I somehow find very annoying.

I finally get home. *Got to clean up the place for renters*, I am thinking. *There is so much to do!*

The rest of the night is a blur. I am cleaning the refrigerator. I am cleaning everything. The inside of the refrigerator looks so white and new that I don't want to leave anymore. Wow!

I call my mother. Her mind is elsewhere, as usual. She has trouble making decisions. She will probably agree with whatever I say. I figure she will be grateful to find renters. Bill and Lucy had said $250 per month would be fair. Mom could actually make a little profit off the place.

"That's nice," says my mother, completely indifferent to my frenzied activity, the fate of her dead mother's mobile home, and the financial implications of all this.

"Listen, Danny." Pause. "I want to die."

"No, you don't, Mom! You're just sad. And besides: it's a terrible sin!"

Is this the true Cry For Help that those after-school TV specials for adolescents had always warned me about? Or is she just a bit sad today? I don't know how to respond. I have no time to ponder such things. I need to call back Bill and Lucy!

"I'll call you back."

I promised I would stop by Aunt Mae and Uncle Myron's to say good-bye. It's already going on 10:00.

Bill and Lucy call before I have any time to gather my thoughts. If am truly leaving, than perhaps they should come over now to check things out. They do. They inspect many things.

"What are you doing with the TV?" asks Lucy, the Great Christian. I blink at her, wondering if she likes to watch the popular sex-innuendo-laden sitcoms.

"I'm just leaving it."

"Well, we need a TV for our bedroom. Would you be interested in selling it?"

"Ah. Sure. You can have it. I mean, you can give me $50 if it works, and just have it if it doesn't work."

"Ok."

I carry it to the car for them. Subconsciously, I feel like I am helping thieves rob me blind. I am exhausted, weak and helpless.

I tell them that my Mom likes the idea of renting to the Cranes. I give them Mom's phone number. I give them a key, so that they can get the place ready if need be. I indicate some things they can throw away if they really need to. I drive home with them around the block to carry the TV in for them. It's quite heavy, and Bill shouldn't strain himself.

Bill drives me home in relative silence. I already feel foolish, as if I'm being swindled by old RLDS Christians.

I go to Aunt Mae and Uncle Myron's to say my final good-bye. They are in their late 80s, and I find their marital banter hysterical to behold.

"Bill and Lucy want the Cranes to live in my Mom's mobile home," I tell them.

"I think that's a terrible idea," said Myron.

"Myron! Where is your heart?!"

"Mae!" he roars, almost sounding like Al Jolson saying "Mammy!" "They've already been kicked out of three other places. They're just a bad risk.

You should never rent to unreliable people. And there's no one here to manage it!" He looks at me. It's clear that he doesn't want to manage it.

"Myron Walsh! Just *when* did you become such a cold-hearted man! And I thought you were a Christian! Don't you ever want to help out anyone?"

"But Mae, Crane's *always* got his hand out. We bought him a car."

Myron also pointed out that the Cranes often had Wendy's mother over to visit. Wendy's mother served as foster mother to five developmentally challenged children. She sometimes brought them to church, and some of the otherwise-loving Christians felt uneasy by the presence of the children, the only black people ever to have stepped into the church.

The five kids saw nothing wrong with getting up and wandering around during a service, or greeting me and a few others vociferously with half-intelligible gestures during even the most solemn parts of the service, all the while being shushed by their adoptive mother for the rock solid hour of church ritual.

"You know they'll be over at the house a lot too," says Myron.

Mae and Myron debate this for a while. Arguing about the future of the mobile home has suddenly taken the spotlight over my final farewell to them—perhaps the last time I would ever see them.

I am tearing up at saying good-bye. Uncle Myron, the hard-working sensible man, has been maybe the best role model I've ever had, better than my own father. Aunt Mae has treated me to countless home-cooked meals and given me all the warmth of a grandmother. They helped put me through college, for God's sake. We warmly say goodbye, and I head home.

I call my Mom. It's about 11:30 p.m. All thoughts of playing the piano one last time are dashed. Now I might not even get a good night's sleep.

"I don't think you should rent to the Cranes, Mom. I know Bill and Lucy want it to happen. But you can't manage it from Cleveland."

"Look, Danny. I- I just don't want to live anymore."

"But Mom. You're like what? Forty-five? You've got lots of time. There's people down here in their eighties still exercising for the future. They're still saving money to go back to Disney World one more time. You've got to get some perspective."

I try my best to be sympathetic, empathetic and comforting. I incant a battery of reasons to live: a catalog, something like Rupert Brooke's poem "These Things I Have Loved." Mom is unmoved.

"Disney World? I've been there," she says.

"Doesn't God make you happy?"

"This isn't God's fault."

"All religions are cults anyway."

"No they're not!"

I remind her again of the joys in little things: fast food, coffee, satisfying work, TV, sex, music. It's of no avail. She's in a black hole of depression. So I try to bring her back to the *terra firma* of property dealings.

"So what do you want to do with your place here?"

"I don't know. What should I do?"

"I don't know."

I hang up the phone around 1:00 a.m. I step outside and take a final look at the black sky and the bright stars of the Florida wilderness. Then I go back inside my dead grandmother's mobile home for my last sleep in Deerwood.

The next day I shook the sand of Disney's Florida from my feet to live in Washington, DC, home of even tougher truths and lies.

About the Author

Dan Geddes is the editor of *The Satirist: America's Most Critical Journal* (www.thesatirist.com), a unique collection of satires, serious reviews, reviews of imaginary works, fiction, essays, and satirical news.

His work has also appeared in the Cleveland *Plain Dealer*, the *Dry Bones Review*, and *The Modern Word*.

Geddes' serious criticism in *The Satirist* online has been widely cited in books, newspapers, academic papers, and websites.

Geddes was born in Cleveland, Ohio in 1970. He studied philosophy and history at Ohio University's Honors Tutorial College and the same subjects, as well as literature, at various graduate schools.

He has also written a novel, a screenplay, a one-act play, and a collection of travel stories.

Geddes enjoys writing, traveling, and playing guitar. He lives in Amsterdam.

Acknowledgements

I would like to thank the following people for their contributions and support.

To Fred: for his great illustrations and unwavering enthusiasm.
To Maria: for proofreading more than once.
To Eric: for his always sharp eye for excess verbiage.
To Diane: for helping me with French.
To Richard: for helping me with German.
To Michael: for appreciating my work so long ago (even the Zen master).
To Nick: whose appreciation for literature has always inspired me.
To Tom: for his close reading and uncannily good judgment.
To Maria, Andrew and Luke: for still loving me despite the time I've lavished on these literary sandcastles.

DG